Contents

I: THE ART OF OVERCOMING FRUSTRATION   1
   Maxwell Maltz   3
   Raymond Charles Barker   16

II: WINGING AWAY FROM FRUSTRATION   33
   Maxwell Maltz   35
   Raymond Charles Barker   49

III: THE ROAD TO SELF-RESPECT   63
   Maxwell Maltz   65
   Raymond Charles Barker   79

IV: HAPPINESS AND UNHAPPINESS   93
   Maxwell Maltz   95
   Raymond Charles Barker   109

V: WINNING OUT OVER CRISES   123
   Maxwell Maltz   125
   Raymond Charles Barker   139

VI: ON TO SUCCESS!   153
   Maxwell Maltz   155
   Raymond Charles Barker   171

I

The Art of
Overcoming Frustration

Maxwell Maltz

Pax vobiscum. Peace be with you. But how do you achieve this peace, this peace of mind which takes you away from your negative feelings, which helps you conquer frustration?

We will study this all-important question and we will analyze the forces you must harness. We will also study the components of frustration and discuss the art of overcoming these negative forces.

Not too long ago I gave a three-day seminar in Salinas, California, and after that another seminar in San Luis Obispo, a lovely little town. At this latter meeting I was quite surprised to see the Warden of the local men's Colony—a penitentiary accommodating over 2,000 people. He was there with his educational staff. We became friends and I visited the Colony—a beautiful place. The men serving time there were learning various trades. We talked about setting up a self-fulfillment program in Psycho-Cybernetics—The Conquest of Frustration. I thought it was a wonderful idea, and we arranged to start it soon.

Two days later I left California and returned home to New York. When I got to my office-home, there was a large envelope addressed to me from the Department of Justice, Bureau of Prisons. I thought: Now what have I done wrong? I opened the envelope. Inside were two letters and a pamphlet. One letter was from the Director of Education of one of the largest Federal penitentiaries in our country, requesting that I come to the graduating exercises of a course in Psycho-Cybernetics they had just completed in the penitentiary. I was amazed, for I didn't even know it existed. There was also a letter from the main teacher, a man who was serving over fifteen years, who has been a marvelous teacher in Psycho-Cybernetics over a period of three years—and I was overwhelmed. He hoped and prayed that I would appear. I immediately wired them that I would be there, and so I participated in the graduation exercises of men who were serving sentences for a long period of time.

And this reminded me of another story; you can find it in greater detail in my book *Creative Living for Today.** It was about a woman named Anna whose three month old infant was torn from her and trampled to death during the Nazi occupation of Poland in 1942. She was thrown into a concentration camp, her husband in another. She thought him dead. Heartbroken, she refused to let her spirit be crushed. She refused to admit defeat when she worked in a slave labor factory. Nothing could destroy her self-respect. The German guards beat her and scarred her face, but she refused to yield to frustration and despair. Eventually she was freed when the Nazis were defeated. Her husband, too, was freed. They found each other again. Her son, born in America, is now studying to be a doctor.

She came to see me at my office, hoping I could remove the scar from her face so that her son could see her as she really was. The operation was successful but the beauty of her face could never match the beauty of her self-image—an image that refused to be buried under the heavy weight of terrifying persecution.

These problems of overcoming frustrations are arresting since the frustrations involved imprisonment. I mention them because they are so illustrative of an imprisonment that is real and physical.

But you are outside of prison—aren't you? Or are you? Is your prison better or worse than an actual prison? Truly, this is debatable. For it is a tortuous prison, an antisocial prison, the prison without, the prison you create inside yourself through frustration, hiding behind locked doors and walking away from the realities of life,

* Trident Press, 1967.

making your Image of yourself shrink to the size of a small potato. Who are you? Are you in prison, or can you be free from the dead weight of negative feelings: This is what the problem is all about, as I see it.

Recently, I spoke in Washington to an assemblage of insurance people—and I saw Washington burn. *Pax vobiscum!* Peace be with you! Where is this Peace, with our country burning? Which is the worse conflagration, the outside one or the fires within us—the hatred, the bigotry, the resentment within us? We hear talk of better policing, but there are not enough policemen to police this world, there are not enough U.N.s to police this world. This business of creative Psycho-Cybernetics is self-fulfillment—peace of mind—and it starts with knowing how to police yourself first. You can't be a friend to others unless you are a friend to yourself. You can't be a success with others unless you are a success with yourself. You can't have the love of others unless you have the love of yourself as SOMEBODY! Somebody capable of blunders, but someone capable of rising above them. The mistake-maker but, thank God, the mistake-breaker. Someone overcome by frustration, yet someone able to rise above—to conquer it.

You wake up in the morning and your day is reality —but what are you preparing to do with this reality?

Oh, how vital are these first few minutes of your day! You look in the mirror. What kind of day is it going to be, Betsy baby? What kind of day is it going to be, Charlie, old boy? You have to make a decision. You see two people in the mirror. You see the person of frustration and you see the person of confidence. Who will win out—inside of you?

Who are you going to be those first few minutes of your day? If you permit some frustration of the past to insinuate itself into your day, you have lost. Your day will be fruitless, self-destructive. On the other hand, suppose you look in the mirror and say: "Betsy baby, Charlie my boy, this is my day. Today I fulfill myself, and even if I fall flat on my face I'm going to stand up and keep punching until I reach my goal." Well! You are reaching out toward utility, toward dynamic living, toward your goals. You are planning success—and even if you don't reach your goals that day, chances are you will reach them another time. The baby who reaches out with open arms to his mother feels a faith that she will answer his need for affection. You, at a later age, must re-awaken in yourself this same kind of deep faith.

In the final analysis, the conquest of frustration depends on you and no one else. No one can make you unhappy without your consent. No one can make you lonely without your consent. No one can fill you with frustration without your consent.

The Displaced Person

Are you a displaced person? Ask yourself—are you? Think about it. Just the other day, I looked in the papers and saw some pictures of the harrowing situation in Vietnam—mothers and children displaced, tragedy written on their faces. Displaced people—almost as bad as during the Nazi occupation. Are you, in spite of your sense of freedom, a displaced person? Ask yourself that. You are displaced if you live in your own prison. You are displaced if you are filled with frustration.

Now, by frustration I don't mean the daily complaints we all have—the normal frustrations we experience during twenty-four hours of living. I'm talking about chronic frustration, piling on your mental back fifty pounds of extra mental and spiritual weight—the old heartaches, the old tragedies, the old guilts, the old misfortunes, the old loneliness of a yesterday which should remain a yesterday.

The conquest of frustration, the quest for happiness, the business of creative living to achieve peace of mind starts with living now. You've got to live now—N-O-W. Forget yesterday, lost in the vacuum of time, buried deep, deep in the tomb of time. The conquest of frustration starts *now!* You must realize this.

Still it isn't worth anything if you don't turn these thoughts into golden opportunities, if you don't transform them into creative performance. In creative performance you've got to be your own plastic surgeon. You have to be your own creative sculptor. Take these thoughts and mold them and shape them into things of

beauty. Use the principles of Psycho-Cybernetics—
which means living in the present and steering your
mind to productive, useful goals.

Let us hear from some people who have used Psycho-Cybernetics as a springboard to better living. Here
is one comment from a man serving a sentence in Leavenworth Penitentiary:

> To say that the use and practice of the principles of
> Psycho-Cybernetics, as laid out by Dr. Maxwell
> Maltz, have been beneficial to me would be a gross
> understatement. Learning to control my emotions
> and not feel anger at all, real or imagined wrong,
> has been the principal achievement I have made by
> studying and using the principles of Psycho-Cyber-
> netics.

Here is another one:

> In preparing myself to re-enter society as a produc-
> tive and useful member, I have in these past four
> years given considerable thought along the lines of
> reestablishing my values and attitudes. Although I
> have learned a beneficial and worthwhile trade to
> support my family, there was still something lack-
> ing. Not being able to put my fingers on it, I enlisted
> in various courses of self-help programs to try to
> fill that empty something within me. . . . I en-
> rolled in a Psycho-Cybernetics Class. As the weeks
> of instruction and study passed, I was pleasantly
> surprised to find that I had developed an Inner
> Peace within myself. Re-evaluating my self-image,
> through conscientious practice of Psycho-Cybernet-
> ics exercises of a positive mental attitude, has filled
> the void in my life. I am now prepared to return to
> society and my family, thanks to Psycho-Cybernet-
> ics.

Are you prepared to return to society? Are you even
part of society? If you are a displaced person through
negative feelings, resentment, frustration, you don't belong to society yet. You will build your concentration

camp a hundred feet tall unless you learn to tear the wall of Jericho down, down, down, so that you can see your image, a true image, an image in God's Image. The whole business of living is to fulfill yourself, to enhance your sense of self-respect. When you do this, you express the God-like quality within you. Are you prepared to stop being a displaced person? Are you prepared to stand on your mental and spiritual feet, opening the doors of the jail into which you put yourself?

Here's another comment:

Since enrolling in the Psycho-Cybernetics workshops, I can honestly and truthfully say there has been a definite change in my mental outlook towards many things. Where I would look on the darker or negative side of things and find only darkness, now I am slowly but surely seeing the brighter side of my everyday life. Use of the principles of Psycho-Cybernetics has helped me in many ways to a better life and a brighter future.

Could you write this—now? Maybe not? Still, let's see how you feel after reading these chapters and then re-reading them.

Now let us consider five roadblocks that lead to frustration:

1. *You worry after you have made a decision.* Worry at times has validity. If you have five ways of reaching your goal and you can't reach the goal taking the five ways, you are anxious. Which road should you take? You must make up your mind. But once you have made your decision, reach out for the goal and fight for it. Then stop worrying about your decision!

2. *You worry about today, yesterday, and tomorrow.* How many of us would like to escape to that lovely island in the sun, forgetting everything, all our tensions, where we could sit under a coconut tree eating luscious coconuts. The opposite of this is constant worry—about today, yesterday, tomorrow—and it leads only to frustration.

3. *You try to do too many things at one time.* You must carefully select your goals, and accept your limita-

tions. Set goals you can achieve, goals you're equipped to achieve. Set reasonable time limits. And you can do many things *at different times*. Julius Caesar couldn't do two things at one time—he did two things at two different times.

4. *You wrestle with problems all day.* If something defies solution, you sleep *with* it, not *on* it. You forget that there are three eight-hour periods to a day—eight hours for work, eight hours for rest and eight hours for sleep. Who asked you to bring the troubles of your office to your home? Who asked you to bring the troubles of your home to your office? You refuse to realize that those middle eight hours are yours, and in these hours you are a king or a queen who can develop pursuits or hobbies to give you pleasure.

5. *You refuse to relax.* You toss and turn on your pillow trying to count sheep jumping through a window. You stay up all night, wondering if you gave yourself the right count. Stop counting. Get your sleep and attack your new day in the morning.

These are your five roadblocks—emotional dead ends that will lead you only to despair.

Now, here is the other side of the coin—four steps on the road to relaxation:

1. *You forgive others.* Oh, how difficult that is! Forgiveness with no strings attached; a clean, clean slate. No forgiveness on the installment plan—the kind that says I love you today, I hate you tomorrow.

2. *You forgive yourself.* This is a human achievement! Alexander Pope said, "To forgive is Divine." We all want to be human, not divine, of course, so let's just try to be human, realizing our capacity for error but also our capacity for rising above it through forgiveness. Forgive others. Forgive yourself.

3. *You see yourself at your best,* as a person of confidence, not as a person of frustration. You must make the decision. No one can make it for you.

4. *You keep up with yourself.* If you try to carry someone else's image, you are beginning to practice frustration. You are beginning to walk into your own concentration camp. You are worse off than many inmates of our penitentiaries.

Five roadblocks to frustration, four principles of relaxation. Stop being a displaced person and start walking out of the jail you have created for yourself.

The Art of Communication

Now—how do you do this? Through the art of communication. How do you communicate? Let me tell you a story.

About a year ago I went to Atlanta, Georgia, to address eight hundred people of the Sales and Executive Marketing Group, celebrating their 25th Anniversary. In honor of the occasion for me, a Yankee from New York coming down to Atlanta, Georgia, there was a young boy named Ray who was fourteen years old. He had a horn and he was going to blow his horn and play "Yankee Doodle" for me. Behind him was a boy, two years older, taller, with a drum. When Ray blew his horn, the other boy would beat the drum. Ray took the horn and put it to his lips. Nothing came out—not a sound. I looked at him, standing there so dejected. It didn't occur to me that the boy had come unprepared to play that song to eight hundred people. I was sure he had practiced for weeks—at least—but he couldn't blow his horn. He couldn't communicate.

He stood there for a while, wondering what had happened. Then he took the mouthpiece off, put a new mouthpiece on, put the horn to his lips. Again nothing came out. My heart went out to this boy in his utter dejection. Defeated, he moved listlessly to a huge round table at the rear of the room where a huge piece of apple pie and cheese and a glass of milk had been set out for him but he didn't see them. He sat, head bowed in shame. And so I got up and I said: "Ladies and gentlemen, the topic of my talk tonight is: 'Ray, who couldn't blow his horn.'"

And I told them about the Ray within every one of us who, because of some fear, panic, or frustration, cannot communicate—cannot blow his horn.

And I also told them the story of another Ray, an eighteen-year-old second-year medical student who wanted to be a doctor and could not recite in class, could not communicate, could not blow his horn.

I was this Ray. When the professor of pathology called on me to quiz me orally, I was in a panic even though I knew my subject. I could not communicate. I thought that the eighty fellow students who looked at me were angry at me, wanted me to fail. And so I did. I sat down defeated. Time after time the same thing happened to me in these oral quizzes.

But I had such a great desire to be a doctor that I refused to let this fear overcome me. I remembered that when I took written examinations, that when I looked through a microscope at a specimen slide I had to identify, when I didn't see the faces of the professor and the students, I was completely relaxed. I wrote down what I saw and got an "A" for my efforts.

I suddenly resolved that the next time the professor gave me an oral quiz, I would make believe I was looking at a slide through a huge microscope and I would pay no attention to my audience. And, sure enough, the next time it happened, I was relaxed, I was confident, I answered properly without hesitation. I cancelled out my fears. I overcame that terrifying feeling of frustration and passed the course with honors.

What am I trying to say? That, like Ray, I, at the age of eighteen, couldn't blow my horn—from panic, from frustration. But I overcame my fears. And if I can do it, you can do it. It doesn't matter if you came from the other side of the tracks. So, too, did I.

Communicate? How do you communicate? Once, before a lecture, a man came over to me and said, "Dr. Maltz, you wrote a terrific book. The men of our insurance agency study a chapter a week, and we get a great bang out of it. Thank you for writing this wonderful book, *Psycho-Ceramics*."

Well, I don't know what Psycho-Ceramics is, but I do know what Psycho-Cybernetics is. Psycho-Cybernetics is the conquest of frustration. Psycho-Cybernetics comes from a Greek word, *kybernetes*, or helmsman, referring to the man who steers a ship to port. And Psycho-Cybernetics means steering your mind to a productive, useful goal. I say that advisedly because, far too often, when we are overcome with frustration, we steer our minds to unproductive, useless, destructive, annihilating goals. Psycho-Cybernetics: steering your mind to a productive, useful goal. When you do that, you can't be frustrated even if you don't reach your goal. For, once you try to reach your goal, you are already there—nothing will stand in your way once you try.

Communication: Through communication you will learn the art of overcoming frustration. But how do you achieve it?

After a lecture to eighteen hundred successful insurance men in Boston, one fellow from Texas asked if he could drive me to the airport to catch a plane to New York.

He said, "Dr. Maltz, I'd like you to do me a favor."

I said, "What is it?"

"I have a son."

"Well, what about your son? How old is he?"

"He's seventeen."

I said, "What's your problem?"

He said, "Doc, I can't communicate with my boy."

I said, *"What do you mean*—you can't communicate with your boy?"

"I just can't."

"Whose fault is it?'

"I don't know."

"What do you mean—'you don't know?' You're the father."

"Doc, I don't want to get into an argument with you. I just can't communicate with my boy and I'd like you to help me. Can you?"

I said, "I don't know if I can, I don't think you'll listen to me. Goodbye, Phillip, I'll see you some other time."

He said, "Come on, try me out."

I said, "I'll tell you what you do. When you get home, you go over to your boy and you say: 'Son, forgive me. It may be that I may have made a mistake about you but isn't it possible that you could have made a mistake about me?' "

I looked at him; he had turned pale.

I said, "You'll never do it. Goodbye, Phillip, I'll see you some other time."

Two months elapsed. I was in my office, busy with noontime patients, my assistants, nurses. One nurse came over to me and said: "Long distance."

I picked up the phone.

"I did it! I did it!" I heard.

"Who is this? You did what?"

"Doctor, it works, it works!"

"What works?"

"Don't you remember me—from Texas?"

I said, "Oh! oh!—just a minute."

I went into an adjoining room where I could listen and this is what I heard: "For two months I couldn't get near my boy and one day we came home from church. He went into the kitchen, chewing on a hero sandwich. I was in my bedroom, chewing on my nails. And then, suddenly, I walked into the kitchen and I said, 'Son, forgive me. It may be that I may have made a mistake about you but isn't it possible that you could have made a mistake about me?' "

Excitedly, he told me that the boy acted as if he was suddenly ten feet tall. He almost crushed his father as he lifted him up in the air. They wept together and felt close, the dearest of friends.

Now, it was love that made this successful businessman communicate. Communicate! How do you communicate? Well, the first principle of communication is that you have to learn how to communicate with yourself. You've got to keep the railroad tracks within you clean and bright, unencumbered by the negative feelings of frustration, inferiority, grief, loneliness, uncertainty, resentment, emptiness. That was yesterday. The business of living, whether you are three or thirty, six or sixty, nine or ninety, is to live. First, you communicate with yourself, then with others. For you can't be a friend to others unless you are a friend to yourself; and you can't be a success with others until you are a success with yourself. You can't receive love from others unless you give love to yourself.

Don't cry in your soup because you failed in some undertaking twenty years ago. That's another lifetime!

You belong to yourself *now*. Forget the time when you incarcerated yourself in your own jail, in your own concentration camp, because you were unhappy over some misfortune.

The business of living, the business of being successful, the business of rising above frustration is to *rise*—above a heartache, a misfortune, a guilt, a negative feeling, a feeling of hatred, a feeling of bigotry.

Finally, let us study what I call The Twelve Faces of Frustration. So you can see them clearly, and win out over them.

So you can make yourself expert in the art of overcoming frustration.

The Twelve Faces of Frustration

1. *You are not true to yourself.* You fail to support yourself with true loyalty.

2. *You use your imagination destructively*—as when you have no goal. If you want to use your imagination positively you must think of a goal, somewhere to go, a goal within your capabilities. Don't try to be the President of the United States—he's got enough trouble. Just be yourself with your own headaches; and the beauty of these headaches is that you can rise above them to a full state of emotional health.

3. *You don't know how to relax.* Your mind seethes with complexities.

4. *Your aim is unhappiness.* Yet happiness belongs to you like your eyes, like your heart, like your pulse. Reach for it, without stepping on other people's toes—without stepping on your own toes with negative feelings.

5. *Frustration is a habit.* You've hypnotized yourself into believing that you can't amount to anything . . . and . . . so you won't. You talk to a child four years of age on the phone and if you're full of frustration, the child will feel it. Positivize your habits!

6. *You don't accept your weaknesses.* But you've got to, for you're only human and you need a floor upon which to stand.

7. *You have no compassion.* With compassion, you are *somebody;* without compassion, you are nobody.

8. *You wear a mask.* You play games with yourself and with other people.

9. *You repeat your mistakes.* You've got to *grow through your mistakes.*

10. *You retire from life.* But no human being, when alive, has the right to do this. I cannot see how you can retire from life without doing yourself a disservice.

11. *You consider yourself a loser.* If you want to conquer frustration, learn the art of the money-player; think like a winner. If you should lose, there's always the next day. Remember that just because you're a loser once doesn't mean you're going to lose forever.

12. *You don't accept yourself for what you are.* You live in fantasy. When you come back to earth, you find it is a frustrating place.

These are The Twleve Faces of Frustration. Face up to them! Outstare them! Win out over them!

If you don't, you will not find happiness—not in this world, not in any world. Money cannot buy it for you; realistic situations of value will find you wanting; people will not give it to you. For happiness at its base is something *you* create from inside *yourself.* Happiness is something *you* give *yourself.*

Let this be your motto. PAX VOBISCUM! Peace be with you.

Raymond Charles Barker

Maxwell Maltz and I have been friends for a good many years and I've learned from experience to respect his sense of humor as well as his integrity. But I did a double-take when he dropped into my office one day and announced: "Raymond, I'm going to jail on Friday."

He was referring, of course, to his visit to the federal penitentiary at Leavenworth, Kansas—a trip he has already told you about. He filled me in on the details by telling how his ideas on goal-striving and self-fulfillment have reached and helped thousands of men behind bars. How the principles of Psycho-Cybernetics have given them hope for the *now* and hope for the future when they are able, once more, to take their places in society.

Frustrations naturally beset men and women who have lost their freedom and spend most of their time locked in prison cells or prison yards. In many cases, I've no doubt, overwhelming frustrations led to their crimes.

But you and I are *physically* free. Nevertheless, we sometimes find ourselves unable to reach a goal we have set our sights on because we are *mentally* locked up. Locked in a prison of our own making. A prison built, bar by bar, by frustrations that we haven't conquered.

I am sure this problem goes way back to primitive man. He struggled to learn the art of speech. He struggled to learn the art of love, moving love out of the category of just a basic sex function into an enduring means of communication. I am sure he struggled with that. There were problems with food, shelter and safety—and many other things. But step by step, primitive man conquered his basic frustrations.

And now modern man—who has also conquered many frustrations—lives in a world of great advancement. A world where positive thoughts and feelings have moved him ahead but where negative thoughts and feelings have held him back.

The process of evolution has been, I believe, a gradual unlocking of many of the doors built up by frustrations, doors that have threatened, but failed, to keep mankind from a measure of self-fulfillment. And as a result, century after century and generation after generation, we, as a people, have become more creative, more self-expressive. We had to do this in order to get where we wanted to go.

That is a race picture, a picture of civilization in general. But what about you and me as individuals? Do you have some goal you haven't reached because you can't stay on the track, because you are fearful, lack self-confidence or feel inferior?

Well, I have a confession to make.

I consider myself a healthy extrovert and I am *unfrustrated* in most things. I certainly am unfrustrated in the pulpit. But I'll tell you about a secret frustration of mine.

Some years ago, a talent promoter came to see me and said: "Barker, you are so good at speech-making that you ought to be out cashing in big money on the lecture circuit." I replied, "Of course, I know I'm good but what does one do? How do I go about it?"

"Don't worry. I'll start you on Rotary Clubs," he told me.

He did. He started me on Rotary Clubs. And what did I do? I fell flat as could be. I managed to talk the necessary length of time but I was not animated. I was dull. This amazed me because I like the Rotarians, a fine organization. I later went before the Elks Club and fell flat there, too.

I am totally free of frustration in the pulpit; but put me in front of a sales convention and I am a flop. Put me in any Church of Religious Science, any metaphysical church in the world, and my message pours forth.

But put me in front of a Women's Garden Club or any group of people not closely related to the New Thought movement, or metaphysical beliefs, and I'm far from a success.

This is an area I should conquer. I should get over this frustration of not being able to speak effectively to nonrelated groups of people. I should quit making excuses that unless the members of the audience have some background knowledge of Religious Science instruction they have nothing within them that will respond to me.

Your own area of frustration may be far different from mine. You may need money for an education or to meet a financial obligation and you may not know how to go about getting the necessary funds. You may hate your boss but want to continue in your job. You may have a responsibility for some relative that keeps you tied down in a small town, when you really want to live and work in a big city.

These are run-of-the-mill frustrations. Many people have them. Basically, they are God-given *urges* to get out of a rut, to move on, to progress. I believe that these frustrations are caused by the universal urge toward evolution that exists in each one of us, the urge to aim ever higher and higher in our achievements. We must remember that you and I are not finished people; we are evolving people. We live in a world of evolving people and we still have a long way to go. If you don't think so, read the daily papers. We, collectively, are the unfinished business of life—still evolving. Individually, we also are unfinished business.

Dr. Maltz has set a scene for us in which you look in the mirror for a few minutes after you awaken each morning. "Which face do you see?" he asks. Which face? Do you see the one that represents frustration, a down-at-the mouth person who thinks the world is against him and knows that nothing is going to go right that day? Or do you see the face that represents confidence? The face that shines with anticipation of worlds to conquer? Small personal worlds, of course, but worlds of great significance to you, the individual.

Now, I am going to interpret those two faces in the

mirror a bit differently. When I look into the mirror, I see what my conscious mind and my subconscious mind have done *with* me and *for* me. The two faces in my mirror represent my conscious and my subconscious mind.

I see the conscious-mind picture of myself as the Raymond Charles Barker whom I see every day. I'm familiar with that face. But the other face, which represents a deep subconscious pattern of myself, may be quite unlike my conscious-mind face; and it is not so readily seen. There may be quite a contrast between the conscious-mind picture and the subconscious-mind picture. It may be as great as the contrast between *confidence* and *frustration*. This all depends on what my self-image is like—or, if *you* are looking in the mirror, what *your* self-image is like.

When we refer to self-images we move right back to the Psycho-Cybernetics field. Remember: You are steering your mind to a productive goal; or, if you are overcome with frustration, you are steering your mind toward an unproductive, useless or destructive goal.

The self-image—the way you really appear to yourself in your own thinking—governs what happens in your life. The pattern of your self-image is firmly fixed in your subconscious mind.

One of the most important things we have learned from Freudian psychology is that in any conflict between the conscious and subconscious mind the subconscious will always win. What you believe yourself to be at the subconscious level is what you really are. The conscious mind has, as one of its many facets, the capacity to create delusion. So I can look into the mirror and delude myself, temporarily make myself believe that I am a better or a greater person that I am—or perhaps a worse person. I can put on a mask and, for a few minutes, I can fool myself. But I'm not fooling my subconscious mind.

The subconscious mind is a storehouse of all your beliefs—or my beliefs. Do you like yourself or don't you? The answer to that question is firmly implanted in your subconscious mind. And you had better like yourself or you'll never be successful in the practice of Psycho-Cybernetics—the conquest of frustration.

I frequently have someone say to me, in a counseling session, "Dr. Barker, how do I go about liking myself when I'm such a failure? When I have no friends?"

After suggesting to this person that he certainly should be able to find some points in his character worth admiring, I advise him simply to say, "I like myself." Say it over and over again—day after day—when no one is around. This is an important first step toward building the image of yourself that you want. When you say, "I like myself," you are planting a seed in your subconscious mind. If you say it enough times, your subconscious will accept it as the truth.

But too few people do that. I'm astounded at the number of men and women with whom I talk who do not like themselves. Maybe they think that's their secret but they give themselves away by continually running themselves down. It is fine to recognize your weaknesses and correct them; or, if you can't do that, to accept them. But merely to complain about them gets you nowhere and indicates that you have a self-image that is steering you toward unhappiness and failure. Perhaps *you* didn't even build this self-image. You may have taken one that someone else gave you.

I frequently ask such a downbeat person: "When you were a child, which parent wanted you to fail? Which parent told you that you would never amount to anything when you grew up?"

There is a moment of embarrassment, and sometimes I see a look bordering on terror on the person's face. *Must I tell him?* that look seems to say. Of course, I never force the issue but I usually get the answer.

In one case it may be a domineering father who has called his slightly-built son a runt or a weakling and declared that he would never be able to handle a he-man's job. In another, we may find a society-minded mother who has constantly bemoaned the fact that her little girl isn't pretty, that she is going to have a hard time finding a husband when she grows up.

Many sons and daughters have accepted a parent's judgment as their own and built their self-images around it. I say to the son or the daughter, now grown to adult-hood: "All right. If you have let this influence your atti-tude toward life, then your subconscious mind is being run by an idea someone else put into it. Let's get that idea out and put your own image of yourself in its place."

I find that this complete acceptance of someone else's opinion often occurs in a marriage relationship. A hus-band or a wife, usually in sarcasm, makes unkind or de-rogatory remarks that are projected into the other per-son's mind as a self-image, a very wrong self-image, but one that may be hard to uproot. A sister or a brother may cause you to have a false image of your real self, if you listen to the judgments that are made and accept the verdict.

There is a great tendency to go back to the little boy or the little girl you once were, to go back to those early years when other people's images of you were put into your mind and, because of their impact, these images stayed there. You see yourself as others saw you. You do not see yourself as the real you that you are.

This is dangerous. It can rob you of your happiness and peace of mind. Say to yourself:

This image is not my image. I don't like it. I have let this image be in me and I have let it operate me. And it is going to stop.

Old-timers at the First Church of Religious Science in New York City know that I quite often say: "I am not George Barker's little boy any more; and I am not Har-riette Barker's boy any more. I now am Raymond Charles Barker, an adult. Both of my parents are on their own pathway. I am an adult—I am myself."

So I talk to myself, as you will learn to do, and I say: "Wrong self-image in my subconscious, you stop! You are neutralized by my right thinking. You come to mind no more. I now declare that in my subconscious mind there is a perfect individual known as Raymond Charles Barker. There is a man made in the image and likeness of God. There is a creative person. I am valuable to life and valuable to myself."

I do this perhaps once every three or four days; I do this because I want *my* mind, not someone else's mind, to run me. Therefore I have to put in my subconscious mind *my* self-image.

I look in the mirror and I see two faces: my conscious-mind face and my subconscious-mind face. I am looking at what I am; and I am looking at that which has caused me to be what I am and that which will cause me to be whatever I may be in the future. I know that my subconscious mind is always in action producing the *me* that I have accepted for myself. So, if I don't like that me, I have to go about the business of changing it.

You can do the same.

Taking a look at the five roadblocks that Dr. Maltz discussed will serve as a starter. However, I am going to work them out from a positive viewpoint.

The first one, you will remember, is *indecision*. Start thinking of yourself as a decision-making person because you are. One of the strongest arguments I make in my recently published book, *The Power of Decision*,* is that indecision is a decision to fail. Indecision is actually that: *It is a decision to fail.*

Check over your life. By this I mean check over your present livingness. You may find that you are very decisive in certain areas and indecisive in others. Forget those where you are decisive because you are in control there. You made up your mind to do something and you did it. Now check the areas where you are indecisive, where you are afraid to say yes or no—I will or I won't. These are the areas where you will need to work to improve.

Let's take an example.

One of the most annoying things that can happen to a host who takes three people to a restaurant is to have to watch those three people with their indecisiveness. It happens to me often. We arrive at the restaurant. I look at a menu and decide what I want to eat. That's one area of consciousness where I have *no* indecision. But I've wasted a lot of valuable time with people who don't know whether they should have this or have that. "What are you going to have, Dr. Barker?" they ask. It's the in-

* *The Power of Decision*, Dodd, Mead & Company, New York.

evitable question. When I tell them, all three of them say, "Well, I'll have the same thing."

I've used this common-variety situation to illustrate a human characteristic that may cause real havoc in the life of a person whose indecisiveness controls most of his behavior. Remember: *Indecision* is a roadblock that makes you take a detour on the way to happiness and success. Watch out. If you are indecisive in one area of your life you probably are indecisive in many others.

I have one friend with whom I refuse to go shopping. Suppose he is only buying a tie. He asks the opinion of whoever is with him. "Do you like this tie?" If the answer is yes, he buys the tie. He takes it home and then, ten chances to one, he returns it to the store the next day. I decided long ago to let this friend do his indecision work on his own time—not on mine.

Your indecisions may be largely concerned with small matters such as I have outlined; or, they may have to do with far more important things, such as changing a job, moving into a new house or even deciding whom you will marry. Watch out for your areas of indecision and *do something* about them. You were born with a mind and a set of emotions. They are your vital equipment; your body is entirely secondary. Use this mind and set of emotions when you make your decisions. You are going to be making them from now on throughout eternity; and you might just as well get started now.

Indecision makes you unattractive to other people. You may lose many friends by your shilly-shallying ways. At least you'll make them impatient and hesitant to seek your company.

I'm sure you know someone like Mary, who, when she's invited to go to the movies, never knows which picture she wants to see. "It doesn't matter," she will say. "Let's go where you want to go." Trying to be helpful her escort asks, "Well, do you like a musical? Or, would you rather see a comedy? Maybe an adventure?" Her answer is, "Oh, I don't really know. I guess one picture is as good as another. You pick the show and I'm sure I'll enjoy it."

The problem is not that Mary doesn't know what she likes. She is just in the habit of indecision and for the rest of her life she probably will avoid making choices. She will never announce to her friends where she wants to go and what she wants to do. But that's not my way of doing it. I *announce*. Yes, I announce.

So, for all the Marys and all the Johns who have read this far and resolved to remove the first roadblock in the conquest of frustration, here is a positive statement I would like you to make:

I am a decision-making individual; I am a decision maker. Once I have made a decision I proceed toward my goal.

Repeat that statement often, especially when you find yourself reluctant to make up your mind.

And be sure that you don't worry about wrong decisions. You have made many of them and you will make many more. They haven't wrecked you and you have learned valuable lessons from them.

As a matter of fact, *worry* is the next roadblock we are going to consider here. It is second on Dr. Maltz's list. Worry is the greatest waste of mental and emotional energy that has ever overtaken the human race on its upward path. And I suspect we have been worrying ever since we first began to know ourselves—that first flash of self-consciousness back there somewhere along the evolutionary path.

I believe one of the reasons why religion always has been important to man is that it has given him a faith symbol—no matter what kind of religion it was. It has helped lessen his worry load. That is why different religions have helped different people. Each has *lessened the worry load*.

Here we are, well past the middle of the twentieth century, and you would think that with everything we have today we would be worrying less. I wonder if we aren't worrying more. I wonder if our accumulation of more possessions and our ability to do more things and to go more places has not increased the worry load rather than decreased it.

What can we do about this tendency to worry about many things? Here is my suggestion to you.

Think of the place, a physical location, where you do most of your worrying. Is it a certain chair in the living room? Is it a chair at your desk? Is it in bed, after you have retired for the night? Figure out your key worry spot. If you drive a car a great deal, maybe the driver's seat is what we might call your anxiety seat.

When you have found your chief worry spot, make a decision that there is to be no more worry there. If you feel that you must worry, go to a different chair. Call it your "faith chair" or "faith spot" if it isn't a chair. After a while you will probably feel so ridiculous that you may start laughing instead of negating.

A good laugh will often remove your tension and put you in a better problem-solving frame of mind. Remember that you are in possession of a great creative instrument—your mind. None of us truly appreciates the intracacy of this mind and the emotions that back it up. We fail to recognize its brilliance. So instead of letting it lead us to our goal, we sometimes take all of this mental and emotional energy and —*whammy!*—we turn it in a negative direction and get negative results.

That's not the way to progress along the pathway of life. In order to be happy and successful, you accept only the good and the positive. When you run into people who say they can't help worrying, remember that this is nonsense. Anyone can stop worrying, unless he or she is a complete neurotic. It takes a bit of doing, of course. It takes finding something you are actively interested in, something that awakens your enthusiasm. When you have challenging goals to achive, the time you allot to worrying is minimized. That's great; worry never solves anything. It is just a roadblock.

Tell your subconscious mind, the Doer within you, that it is to stop bothering you. Here is a positive statement for you to make:

I am not a worry person. I am a right-thinking, creative individual, valuable to life.

Failure to do what needs to be done is our third roadblock. Dr. Maltz speaks of the importance of doing one thing at a time, not trying to do too many things at once. Naturally, if you are going to do one thing at a time, you will do the most important thing first. And if you sit around and put off doing anything, you place yourself in the class of the eternal procrastinators. Procrastination is a habit—that's all it is. It happens to be a very wrong habit. It is a habit you do not have to change unless you want to. But if you will look at the records of men and women who have won success in some field of endeavor, you will discover that none of them procrastinated in his or her chosen work. Some of these successful individuals may have been procrastinators about taking out the laundry or such trivia but in their chosen arena of success there was no procrastination. Whatever *needs* to be done is done by the successful person.

In our former church building, when we were without adequate help, I would do the vacuuming. It didn't bother me to mop a floor. I wouldn't do it in my own apartment. But I would do it for the church, because the church was my success idea. When you have true motivation for success, you will not procrastinate in that area. If you are a procrastinator, do something about it.

The cosmic order—of which you are a valuable part —is always on time. It gets done what needs to be done at the instant it needs to do it. You can consult a meteorologist at the United States Government Weather Bureau and he can tell you the exact time the tides will come in tomorrow or on a certain day next week or next month. Those tides, operating on exact schedule today, undoubtedly will be operating on exact schedule a million years from now. The meteorologist can predict exactly what time the sun will rise each morning and set each evening during the present year; and the sun is expected to be on time for all the years to come.

The cosmic process is always on time. You are part of this process. You are cosmic process individualized as you, and you can be on time. Start saying:
I am an on-time individual, and I do what needs to be done in order to be a success.

If you really are a success person you will know what an important key point our next roadblock is—*insoluble problems.* You probably have friends and neighbors who insist that their problems are too grave, or too complicated, to be solved. They go around announcing this, discussing the problem in question *ad infinitum*. But that's as far as they go.

There is not a problem in the universe that cannot be solved. The insoluble problems of a hundred years ago have, for the most part, been solved. Those of a hundred years from now will be solved in their own time. So who are you and I to sit back and say that our problems can't be solved?

Every problem is the result of an idea; and every solution is the result of another idea. All ideas come to us from on source—the Infinite Creative Mind. If you believe that source and trust that source, you will be guided to the right answer no matter how serious your situation may seem. But when you take a negative attitude and say something cannot be done, you are planting in your subconscious mind a belief in failure. You are blocking the channels that let inspired thinking come through.

Start saying to yourself:

Every problem I have in my world today can be solved because my mind is intelligent. I have the intelligence of the Infinite Mind within me and when I expect this intelligence to act and give me right ideas, it does. But as long as I sit around declaring that I have a problem that can't be solved, I am really saying that I do not have enough intelligence to find a solution. Every problem in my world today can be solved.

You magnify and give power to problems when you dwell on them. The first thing you learn in this teaching is: Diminish the power of any negative; cut the power down. You cut the power down by giving the problem less attention, less importance and by saying:

I can beat this. I can beat it. There is an answer. The answer is in my mind right now and it reveals itself in my mind right now. There are no insoluble problems.

The fifth and last of Dr. Maltz's roadblocks is: *We refuse to relax.* He has given you some specific instructions on how to relax. But I believe all of us must first get over the idea that it is necessary to hurry and scurry through life. It is fashionable these days to be too busy; it is fashionable to always be tired; it is fashionable to feel that you are overworked; it is fashionable to feel that life today is complicated.

I wish you could move back in time and follow a typical grandmother, perhaps of your grandmother's generation, when she lived on a farm in Iowa. The water was outside the house—not inside. She pumped it from a cistern or well and carried it in a bucket into the kitchen. She often milked the cows and fed the pigs; she also tended the garden. On her hands and knees, she scrubbed the floors until they were spotless and she baked the most wonderful bread.

There were no soap-filled scouring pads, no detergents. She often made her own soap from her special recipe. Lighting, usually by means of a kerosene lamp, was inadequate and Grandma had no electrical equipment. If you were to follow her around for one day you would drop from exhaustion. So when you think that life today is too complicated, remember Grandmother.

Life today may be *just as* complicated for all of us as it was in the so-called "good old days" but it is *no more* complicated. Now if you are concentrating on your own life, and saying that it is too complicated, what are you doing to simplify it?

Are you wasting time with people who add nothing to your livingness? "Friends" who are just hangers-on? Who contribute nothing to your happiness? Then get rid of them and cultivate a close relationship only with the people who bring meaning and pleasure into your day-to-day living.

I know that I have precious little time to waste on stupid people, men and women whom I do not enjoy. You will never hear me say, "I am going to take so-and-so to the theater because I ought to." Either I like the person or I don't go. I have also ended my duty trips to relatives, and *old friends of Mother's*. They are forever coming to New York and you don't know how busy I can be when I get the name over the telephone. All tied up! Sorry. I would rather read a good book than waste time on uninteresting people.

However, it may not be the other fellow who makes it impossible for you to relax. Maybe it is you yourself. Many people are afraid of a brief period of silence—of aloneness—because they don't want to face up to what they may find out if they commune with themselves. By staying overwrought, busy, hèctic, they don't have to comtemplate the inner workings of their minds. They put the blame for their frustrations on the office; on the home; on the pressure of social events; or maybe on the nasty weather.

You and I need to face ourselves. Do you know why? You'll find that if you look within yourself you are really quite a nice person. You do not have to dodge the truth about yourself. Every mistake you have made is one that I have made in a different way. Your next-door neighbor has made it and probably several people down the street, whom you don't even know, have made it. So don't let the fear of getting to know your real self keep you from relaxing.

Try five minutes without the radio, without television, without a magazine, without a book—and sit in a comfortable chair. Say to yourself: "I'm going to do nothing for five minutes." Of course, your mind will think of twenty things that you ought to be doing. I learned to do this recently. Two or three times a week, I sit down, away from a desk and in a chair I don't usually sit in. I sit down and say, "I'm going to do nothing for five minutes."

My mind starts to hurry and bustle. What will happen if the phone rings? If it rings, it rings; I won't answer it. What will happen if the doorbell rings? It will ring; I won't answer it. Well, maybe they are delivering something important. They can deliver it later. I argue with myself but I do nothing for five minutes and, eventually, I feel relaxed.

Take a chair and call it your "do-nothing chair." Sit down in it and let your mind wander. You can't stop thinking, of course, so this is a good time to do some *creative thinking*.

What is creative thinking?

To those who are familiar with metaphysical teachings, or the teachings of Religious Science, the term needs no explanation. But for some readers who are bound to ask that question, here is a simple explanation.

We are not merely referring to the artist, the writer

or the inventor who thinks creatively and creates. We are referring to you; to anyone who sets a goal and strives to reach it. Visualize that goal as you relax. Picture it in your own mind and see how you will look when you have achieved it; where you will be and what you will be doing. Imagine that you have already reached that goal and feel the exultant emotions; experience the joy that goes with obtaining something that is your heart's desire.

When you create this picture you are actually planting a seed—an idea—in the subconscious mind, and if you believe that the subconscious mind can carry out your desire once you have made it known, you have started on your way to self-fulfillment. Visualizing your goal for five relaxing minutes each day is a powerful way to attain it.

Dr. Maltz has pointed out that an important factor in the art of relaxing is *forgiveness*. This includes forgiving others and forgiving yourself. How do you do it? Just by saying, "I forgive."

I do this when I am alone. I say: "I forgive every person in my life from the day I was born to the present. I forgive everyone who has hurt me down through the years. I forgive; I bless you. You have cluttered up my mind much too much. You have caused me to waste my mental and emotional energy thinking about the hurts. I've got too much to do to carry you around any longer. I'm a busy man. I have a goal and I am going to get there; and I cannot get there if I am worried about some dreadful thing someone said to me five years ago." Then I add: "Subconscious mind, you do the rest of the work." And it does.

Then there is the point of forgiving yourself. You and I carry a pretty heavy guilt load, you know, concerning things we didn't do and things we did do. Every time we can lessen that load we are on the road to what we want.

So I say: "All right, Barker, you now forgive Barker for all the stupidities, minor and major, that your subconscious mind can remember you've ever committed. You now forgive yourself. You can't carry that old load around either."

When you have forgiven others and forgiven yourself, you might ask yourself this question: "Am I able to give myself away?"

The key word here is communication. Can you communicate well with other people? You see, communication is the ability to give yourself away. People who are noncommunicative are afraid to do this. There is a fear of discovery back of the lack of communication; a fear that the person with whom you communicate will find out something about you that you don't want him to know—maybe something that is not very nice. You think that if you are noncommunicative, no one will find out your secret.

When you give yourself away—give of yourself to others—you will probably discover that your close friends and your loved ones know far more about you than you think. I don't believe that a man who has a smart wife can keep any great secrets from her. And I doubt if a woman who has a smart husband can keep very many secrets from him either.

Now, how do we give ourselves away through communication? When I'm talking with you, I am giving of myself to you, whether it be in a public place or whether it be shaking hands and saying "Good morning" to you in the lobby of the church. Communication is a subconscious freedom to give of yourself to others. You may have it in certain areas but not in others.

Make notes of the areas where you do have communication—such as with loved ones, with close friends but not with strangers. Or you may have total communication in the office but not in your social life. Find the areas where you don't have communication and try to figure out what is the secret in those areas that you don't want anyone to discover. What is it that you don't want that particular group to know about you? When you have discovered that secret, sit back and say, "What difference would it make?"

Communication over a broad field, with many people, is an important factor in your happiness and your success. It is part of the conquest of your frustrations—a vital function in your life.

II

Winging Away from
Frustration

Maxwell Maltz

Let us continue our very noble, very worthwhile enterprise—conquest. Not conquest of foreign lands, not conquest in the name of fatherland or motherland, not conquest for gold or treasure. A noble conquest—the conquest of the frustration that eats us.

This conquest—of frustration—is not despotic. It is liberation. Our aim is to enrich our lives, to increase our worth as human beings.

I mentioned that recently I was in Salinas and San Jose, California. In each place I spoke to about two thousand people—maybe more. I was also in San Fransisco where I spoke to three thousand people. I bring this out because of a letter I received from one of the prisoners who heard me speak at Leavenworth. After reading it, I knew that this one person—this prisoner—was more important to me than the thousands I spoke to on that lecture tour.

Here is the letter:

I am a convict at Leavenworth Prison, who has had a very pleasurable first in his life. I am presently reading *Psycho-Cybernetics*. I never had the pleasure of seeing or hearing a great author. Dr. Maltz, I think you are a great plastic surgeon, great author, great public speaker,—and a very great humanitarian. Because of your visit, I have a better insight of myself than ever before. With your book *Psycho-Cybernetics,* the rest is up to me. You have a very fine way of throwing the problem up to a man, and then telling him how to solve it. Dr.

Maltz, what do you think would happen if every literate person in the world could simultaneously read Psycho-Cybernetics? My mind cannot comprehend the total possibilities in human relations for progress. Progress needs to be worldwide now, probably more than at any other time.

I would personally like to thank you and all the people of New York and here in Kansas who are responsible for enabling you to speak to us. I am a better man for the experience, and it would help greatly to balance the ledger of bad experience in my life. The ledger, might I add, is of my own making.

May I thank you greatly and send the best wishes possible to you and all of yours for a long, happy life.

This man, to me, is tremendously significant. We have talked about people in jail and of the many factors that force people to be less than what they are; and here, in one fell swoop, you see a man who, with all the odds against him, shut away in prison, expresses his desire to make something of himself.

Are you, too, in jail? Have you thrust yourself into your own jail?

Have you announced your own jail sentence, by practicing frustration?

Put bars around yourself?

Pronounced your own feeling of inferiority?

Have you rejected yourself?

Eliminated yourself from life?

Refused to pardon your own jail sentence, because you have no sense of forgiveness?

If you have put yourself in jail, you must first realize what you have done—the destruction of your self-image. Then you can embark on a campaign of rehabilitation.

Let me tell you two little stories: After a recent lecture, a young woman came up to speak to me. She was attractive, with a pretty face and a nice figure—but she was obviously burdened with frustration and negative feelings. She told me—now read this carefully—that she felt invisible. In other words, she thought so little of herself that she felt invisible. Many people feel this way and, in a sense, she was fortunate in that she could articulate this feeling. This gave her a chance to tackle the problem head-on and try to deal with it. If you are filled with negative feelings and frustration, you do feel invisible because you think you are nobody.

You can overcome this feeling with more positive images of yourself, when you see in your mind your past successes and see in your imagination your good moments, picturing yourself as the kind of person you admire. Use the technique of money-players in sports: they think they're out to win, and even if they lose, they start punching again in the next contest—always out to win.

Here is another ancedote. In southern France, where I vacationed not too long ago, I was sitting on the beach near the Mediterranean. Nearby, I saw two men on a stone jetty, about to go fishing. They were in their thirties and, from their conversation, I gathered that they were good friends. They both rolled up their trousers and began to fish. One fisherman got a bite quickly and smoothly and reeled in his fish. And then, to my surprise, the other fellow—in anger and frustration—just quit. Furious that his friend caught the first fish, he just quit.

Don't laugh at this story, for, in doing so, you are expressing the tragedy of this man; because laughter is a release, by which you thank God that you're not in that position. It's like your laughter when you see a person slip on a banana peel and fall. You're saying, "Thank God that I'm not in his position." So don't laugh at the tragedy of this man who quit.

You should never make success dependent on another person. It should be up to you, *entirely* up to you. Suppose this man had been alone; he would have been more patient. But his friend beat him to the punch, so he just gave up.

Often, people out of hurt feelings of frustration give up in the game of life, and they stop fishing for success because they envy other people who out-compete them. But real success is based on what you can do with your own life, without worrying about others. When you reach success, your next step must be to help others share it, so they can join in your happiness. Because happiness, in the true sense, is the only commodity in the world that multiplies by division. The more you hand out, the more you have.

There is a little island off the coast of British Columbia whose stony crags are inhabited by a certain species of bird, called a "puffin." It's a tufted small bird—a tufted puffin. The most amazing characteristic of this bird is its habit of living in that spot only. Take it away from that spot and it perishes. It has no resistance, it cannot overcome frustration. It just *dies* if you take it away. This tufted puffin is so fragile that it cannot endure stress.

What kind of bird are you? Are you a tufted puffin . . . with sawdust stuffin'? What kind of bird are you? A mess . . .with stress? Or are you a goal-striver, a stress-survivor. For that's what success is all about. And if you don't survive stress, you are filled with frustration. *What kind of bird are you?* You are a bird; you have wings, symblically speaking.

There is a poem by Victor Hugo, entitled *Wings*.

> *Be like the bird that,*
> *Pausing in its flight awhile*
> *On boughs too light,*
> *Feels them give way,*
> *Yet sings!*
> *Knowing she hath wings.*

Your Wings

Do you have wings? Of course you have. Your wings are your faith and your belief in yourself. And you can *soar* to your destination, if you'll only give yourself a chance. Through frustration—and despair—you clip your wings, and you cannot get off the ground; you cannot even get to first base.

What kind of bird are you? A stuffed puffin? Or can you, with wings of faith and belief, *soar* to your destination? I believe you can; you have to believe it, too.

The letter I received from prison had the prisoner's number on the back of it. It reminded me of the time, a few years after the Second World War, when a woman —a middle-aged woman—came to my office. She wore a peculiar dress with long sleeves, out of fashion completely; and I could tell by the look of her that she carried some heavy burden. When she rolled up the sleeve of her dress, I saw a tattooed number on her arm.

She had been in a concentration camp. She had lost her family—her parents, her husband, her children. And many times, here in New York, she had thought of committing suicide, but something made her go on. She came to my office to have the tattooed numbers removed because she had met a man, a machinist, and she now felt she could have a new life in the northern part of the state. I operated on her; she's now happily married and has a number of children.

Have you a tattoo on your arm? Think of it. Have you? Take a look. You may say, 'No.' But I mean your mental and spiritual arms. Have you tattooed numbers on them? Many of us have; and you, and you alone, can remove these tattooed numbers by having compassion for yourself, by believing in yourself. The man in Leavenworth, Kansas, has a number; you have a number, too, if you're filled with frustration. You must remove these numbers from the skin of your spirit—through belief in yourself, through compassion, through understanding.

When I began to practice—more than forty-five years ago—as an intern I delivered my first baby. I was horrified when the father fainted. The child had been born with a hole in the lip, a harelip, and I felt it was my fault. I was overcome with remorse, and the father had fainted out of remorse, too. Subsequently, I explained to him that we could do something about it. There was a plastic reconstructive surgeon in those days who could correct the deformity. It was this experience that helped me decide to enter the field of plastic surgery.

In my practice I have, of course, operated on harelips. During and after World War II, I taught surgeons in many Latin American countries how to perform such operations on children with this disfigurement.

In one country, a boy of seventeen came to the capital from the interior. He had a harelip since birth and when he was about to be put under anesthesia, he shouted: "I'm going to die! . . .I'm going to die!"

I told him that I was his friend and that he would be all right.

He tried to be calm but I saw the terror in his eyes. Finally, the anesthetist put him to sleep and I repaired the hole in his lip.

Two weeks later the final dressing was removed, and I said to him: "Take a look at yourself in the mirror."

He hesitated. I urged him.

"Don't be afraid."

That minute, before he slowly walked to the mirror, must have been a lifetime to him. Finally, he looked— and stared at himself in disbelief. I knew what was running through his mind. He saw someone he had never seen before. He turned his head in different directions as he kept looking at his new face. Finally, he turned to me with tears of joy in his eyes, and cried:

"I'm going to live! I'm going to live!"

Are you going to live? Have you an emotional harelip? Have you a harelip in your mind? In your spirit? Because of some frustration, where there is a gap between you and your integrity, where there is a hole between you and your dignity as a full-fledged human being? Many of us have. You must remove that gap. Be your own plastic surgeon, and with a little belief in yourself, with a little compassion for yourself, and bridge that gap between you and your dignity with the threads of human kindness.

Who are you? You've got to make up your mind who you are; no one can make it up for you. Your potential rests within you, not within anyone else. *The great escape!*

The prisoner who wrote me has no intention of escaping. He has committed an antisocial offense; he knows he has to serve his time before he can leave.

But how about you? Are you going to build on your great opportunity for your escape? You're not antisocial, but those who practice frustration are antiself. The strange thing about your escape is that, whereas the world is not anxious for a convict to escape, the world is waiting for you to escape—back to yourself. They're rooting for you because the world needs you as a full-fledged balanced human being. The world needs you in these troubled times, in your own serach for peace, which you can't give others unless you feel it yourself.

One of the terrible aspects of frustration is that, because of hurt feelings, remorse, distress, loneliness, hatred, people can easily develop misunderstanding of each other.

The Tomorrow Illusion

So, in this terrible burden of negative feelings, one of the characteristics of frustration is that we like to say—since we are ashamed of our self-image—we like to say: "Well, when tomorrow comes, things will be better; perhaps I'll help myself then."

Most of us are experts at tomorrow-type thinking. We don't need any pre-schooling for that. Too many of us are born that way . . . or else acquire it very quickly. "It's too hot, I'll do it tomorrow." When we have these negative feelings of frustration, we're always pinning the blame on someone else, and we usually say, "Well, in the south—South America—it's too hot, so they're the worst offenders." But you don't believe it; you can have offenders in Scandinavia, too, let alone here.

As members of "Mañana, Inc.," we leave things till a tomorrow that is mostly illusion. For frustration is the thief of time. You cry in your soup, lament the status quo, tell the world you have been wounded, and do nothing about it.

The business of living, the business of overcoming frustration, is to live *now*. Now is the time for self-fulfillment. Not tomorrow, but today.

Still, if you want to do things tomorrow, you can. Some things should be put off till tomorrow. When resentment strikes you, when hatred strikes you, when bigotry strikes you, look in the mirror and say: "Charlie, old boy; Betsy, baby, wait till tomorrow. I'll give vent to my anger, my resentment, my hatred—tomorrow." This is the only time you can be a real expert in the art of self-fulfillment, when you forget these negative feelings, these destructive forces that put a convict number on your mind—on your body—that give you an emotional harelip.

And have a little compassion for yourself. You're only human; you're neither superior nor inferior. You came into this world to succeed, not to fail.

Any doctor who has brought a child into the world —who has spanked it and has heard the cry of life for the first time—could not ever believe that this child came into the world in sin. This child came into the world to succeed, not to fail. You, too, have a moral responsibility to succeed, not to fail. And you begin to succeed when you stop harping on your failures.

You have imagination. It's not just the gift of the poet, the philosopher, the musician, or the sculptor. Still, use your imagination as a sculptor would, chipping away the negative feelings that steer you away from the world. Chip them off your self-image, so your image can shine —an image in God's Image.

A woman baking a roast for her family uses her imagination creatively; she's going to make her family and friends happy. A man who visits a person in a hospital sickbed uses his imagination creatively; he wants to help someone less fortunate. And these are tremendous goals. Yet so many people feel unworthy if they are not world-famous. They don't realize that they can be great in their own right, within their own limitations, if they use their imagination creatively, avoiding frustration and heartache. Because no one can make you feel frustrated without your consent; no one can make you feel unhappy without your consent.

On the other hand, imagination-minus is fear, frustration, no goals.

So how do you overcome frustration? You make a road map of yourself, where you're going and what you want to do. You have a blueprint of yourself—as you look in the mirror. You must decide, on your own terms, what you want to do. Your blueprint is your opinion of yourself; if it's no good, you will fail. If you have an image within your capabilities and you sustain yourself through determination, you'll probably reach your goal.

Your image of yourself, your opinion of yourself—this, of course, is all-important. This opinion of yourself, this will make you or break you. You can't respect others unless you respect yourself. You can't admire others unless you admire yourself. You can't help others unless you help yourself.

When you have a true regard of yourself, you feel a sense of humility—with confidence. You pass on your knowledge to less fortunate people. You give your compassion to other people, your understanding to other people, your sense of direction to other people. You are on your way to worthwhile destinations

Your self-image is the stranger within you simply because you know so little of him. Yet this stranger can be your best friend if you make it your business to get to know him better. You rule him; you can make him what you want him to be—an image of success or an image of failure.

Other Aspects of Frustration

Frustration means your refusal to reach self-fulfillment.

1. You refuse to concentrate on a strong self-image.
2. You refuse to offer it partnership in your life.
3. You refuse to nourish it, thinking it is not basic to your happiness.
4. You refuse to create a proper climate in which it can grow.
5. You refuse to enhance the stature of your dignity as a human being.
6. You refuse to enforce your sense of self.
7. You refuse to develop a proper self-image every day, forgetting that only your true sense of self can make you strong.
8. You refuse to realize that you came into this world to succeed—that you can improve your self-image.
9. You refuse to reactivate the success instinct, the success-mechanism within you.
10. You refuse to have a worthwhile goal. You re-

fuse to understand your needs—to use the courage hidden within you—compassion for yourself. You refuse to play ball with your self-respect—your confidence and self-acceptance waiting to be tapped for the great adventure in self-fulfillment.

These aspects of self-denial produce the following:

1. F *Fear*. This destructive negative feeling arises when you have no goal, when you are continually criticizing yourself, harping on your grievance that the world has been unkind to you. How much more creative it is to turn your back on the fears of yesterday and concentrate on a worthwhile goal today.

2. A *Aggressiveness*. Frustration produces aggressiveness of the wrong kind. You step on other people's toes to get somewhere, not realizing that in this process you get nowhere, not realizing that you are stepping on your own toes, making the road to achievement impossible. The only time you can be aggressive creatively is when you have a goal and reach for it with determination and persistence, refusing to let others steer you away from your course.

3. I *Insecurity*. Frustration produces insecurity. You feel inadequate and inferior. You forget that a mistake does not make you a failure, that no one can make you feel inferior without your consent.

4. L *Loneliness*. Frustration brings loneliness. You feel separated from others and, far worse, you feel separated from yourself. You walk away from reality into the dark tunnel of your troubled mind—alone—without purpose. Remember that no one can make you lonely without your consent.

5. U *Uncertainty*. Frustration means uncertainty. You can not make a decision to be better than what you think you are. Remember we came into this world in uncertainty, we live in uncertainty and we pass on in uncertainty. Remember, also, that the business of creative living—the whole principle of Psycho-Cybernetics—is to bend uncertainty to your will, fulfilling the generic innate desire of every human being to live and be happy. If you remember this goal, common to all mankind, you will fight for it and overcome your uncertainty.

6. R *Resentment*. Resentment is almost synonymous

with frustration. You hate others, blame others for your inadequacy, let others run your life, complaining you never had good fortune. You forget that you, and you alone, can change your luck by turning your back on negative feelings, and by recalling the confidence of past successes as you try to reach your goal in the present.

7. E Emptiness. Frustration ends in emptiness when you say to yourself that you've had it, when you give up on life, shun responsibility, give up on creative goal-striving and leave your destiny to others. Symbolically, you have packed your self-image in a valise, placed the valise in a locker at an airport, locked it—and thrown away the key.

Thus, chronic frustration produces the seven aspects of the failure-mechanism.

Overcoming Frustration

Remember how destructive frustration can be. Remember that it is within your power to make a change for the better . . . to change your self-image. With a little compassion for yourself, by realizing that you are *somebody* of importance—to yourself, to your family, to your community, to your country, to the world—you can be a sculptor of your own spirit and make the diminutive image of yourself grow ten feet tall.

That's what Psycho-Cybernetics is all about. Steering your mind to productive, useful goals. Not steering your mind to unproductive, futile goals through frustration.

A few more words on fear. If you're afraid a burglar will break into your home, you pick up your telephone and call a locksmith. He'll send an expert over to put in some locks to give you protection.

But, on another level, you must not lock yourself up. You must not imprison yourself. You must free yourself to set goals and pursue them, without blocking yourself with fear.

To overcome frustration, you must learn to handle your fear constructively. For, while fear can be valuable, if it's in the form of goal-oriented anxiety, unchanneled, uncontrollable fear means agitation without any purpose. It means retreat from the better side of yourself. The fearful person has succumbed to amnesia; he has lost his dignity, his identity, his potential.

To overcome frustration, you must learn to handle your resentment constructively. You must learn to channel your destructiveness into positive pursuits.

When you carry with your dreams of retaliation, TNT-type of hostility, you're carrying fifty pounds of extra mental weight on your back. Everyone has troubles, problems, complaints. You must transform your destructive goal of disbelief into a constructive goal of belief, transformed from hostility to love. Love of self, first, before you dare offer this love to someone else. And, again, by love, I mean self-respect. When you're filled with frustration, you have acquired a certain guilt, a sense of shame. This sense of shame leads you to resentment and to all these negative feelings that steer you away from reality, from loved ones, from your goals. You must take your chances in life. If you fail, you must learn not to resent yourself.

We rise above feelings of resentment—toward self and others—by accepting ourselves for what we are; by realizing that we are capable of being better people. We must adjust to error, search for our dignity—through compassion.

Compassion is soothing balm for the world-weary. When you give yourself compassion, you give yourself a chance to improve yourself. You refuse to let your mistakes defeat you. You say to yourself, "I am only human." I still like myself.

You keep searching for the better you. You search to make money, which is fine. You search for success—but too often we have a spurious idea of what success is. We think in terms of prestige symbols that produce resentment: Anna has a fur coat, Suzy must have one. John has a Cadillac, Bill has to have one. These prestige symbols mean nothing. You must realize that you are more than a prestige symbol, that success means more than money, that it involves a sense of direction, a quality of understanding and a considerable degree of self-acceptance. As a success, you accept yourself for what you are; you don't try to pretend you're someone else.

Like the athlete who is a money-player, you think of the times when you were a winner, yet knowing from your mature perspective that you'll never be a champion 100 percent of the time. And you refuse to let defeat humiliate you in any way. You accept life's setbacks, realistically; you do not let them throw you.

Finally, a short assignment. See if it doesn't help you.

When you get home, even if someone is looking and thinks you're crazy, sit down with a pencil and a pad and write down something like this:

What did I forget today? Did I forget to aim at being a better person? Did I forget to conquer obsessive fears that make my life miserable? What did I forget today? Did I forget to curb my over-aggressiveness? Did I forget to fight my feelings of insecurity, of loneliness, of uncertainty? What did I forget today? Did I forget to eliminate my resentments? Did I forget my resolve that I would try to be more accepting? What did I forget today? Did I forget to be honest with myself? Did I forget to try to understand the needs of other people, as well as my own? Did I forget to strengthen my self-respect. What did I forget today?

Now, don't blame yourself if you were forgetful today. The important thing is: *did you do your best?* What did you remember to do? What goals did you achieve?

Don't expect yourself to be perfect. You do your best and this you accept; what you forgot to do is human error. Forgive yourself your omissions.

And, then, tomorrow you will set new goals and you will not forget so many. You will build day upon day, week upon week, improving yourself as a human being.

Until frustration is no longer a way of life.

Until you use your wings to fly with your rising spirit.

Until you use your wings to rise above your mental roadblocks.

Until you use your wings to overcome frustration as a mechanism of death.

Then you will say goodbye to The Twelve Faces of

Frustration and to the other aspects of frustration that mean FAILURE.

Then you will say "hello" to life.

This could be the most important adventure of your life. The one you cannot lose. The one for the championship. The one with the high stakes. The one that determines the quality of your life, that spells out your real value as a constructive human being.

Raymond Charles Barker

You and I are mental people and, at one time or another, we have all had the experience of putting ourselves into mental prisons such as Dr. Maltz has described. Yes, in spite of the fact that I am a clergyman, I occasionally do incarcerate myself by allowing hurts, anxieties, or resentments to invade my thinking. Only *I* can do this to myself; no one else can do it to me. When I become frustrated over some situation, be it large or small, it is because I allow myself to build up negative attitudes about that situation. I am sure that I do this without intent, certainly without deliberateness. It is an unconscious welling up in my mind of potentially destructive ideas that I don't bother to check when they should be checked and eliminated.

At such times I let my fears or my worries linger too long in my subconscious. I give them a chance to take root and grow. You should never let disturbing thoughts or emotions last more than two or three hours. Just as a seed planted in fertile soil reproduces its own kind, negative thoughts, if allowed to remain in the subconscious, will eventually create negative, or unhappy, experiences.

If you have repeatedly, over a period of years, allowed attitudes of distrust, envy, hate, or self-doubt to control your thinking, you are indeed imprisoned in a jail of the mind. Your vision has become blurred and distorted; you cannot see clearly while looking out through prison bars. You cannot see yourself, your friends, or your loved ones in the proper light. You are certainly getting a false picture of your own experiences.

A deeply frustrated person, looking at the world with

a warped mind, sees a world of torment, a vast field of unhappiness. This must be changed! Such a person needs to find the means of letting down the bars and unlocking the prison doors. He or she needs to find the key to freedom and a new kind of livingness. That key is positive, creative thinking that helps the dynamic self-image emerge.

You can use your conscious and deliberate thought to plant right ideas in your subconscious. Then you will begin to experience the livingness that is *self-fulfillment*. I call it the sense of making one's own experience rich in living, by means of one's own mind. Attaining this mind control is a one-man job. I can't achieve it for you, and you can't achieve it for me. Furthermore, neither of us can do it unless we know in quiet confidence that we can. When we know, and have faith, the subconscious mind goes to work on the positive ideas we have planted there.

In my book, *Treat Yourself to Life,** which explains how to use scientific prayer, called spiritual treatment in Religious Science, I say: "The basis of scientific treatment is that your subconscious mind is a part of the mind of God. Your subconscious mind is your best friend, your creator, your ally. It will go to work for you at this instant to produce all the joy, all the love, all the peace in your world that you can possibly want. Being a part of the infinite mind, it plays the leading role in the creative process. It is the part of the universal mind which is a law as unchanging and unrelenting as the law of gravity."

This is absolutely true. The trouble is that the average frustrated person has lost the ability to believe that he can become anything better than he is. He doesn't let his subconscious work for him on the positive side; by his negative thinking he forces it to work on the negative side. His self-image is one of self-doubt and low self-esteem. He has firmly implanted in his mind the "poor me," or the "no-one-understands-me" concept. He is busy finding excuses and constructing alibis for his fail-

* *Treat Yourself to Life*, Dodd, & Mead & Company, New York, p. 9.

ures. He has no time to envision successes. In fact, he has lost sight of the thing that he really is.

And what is he? What are each and every one of us? We are *potential*. We have within us the possibility and the capability of becoming anything we want to be, if only we believe in the power of our minds and that of the Infinite Mind working and expressing through us. Once we have achieved our goal—become the person we want to be—we have achieved self-fulfillment. We are successful in some special area, and we are proud of our success. Of course, life is a process of *being* and *becoming;* there is no final achievement and there will always be new goals to attain.

You have probably read some of Dr. Maltz's books and some of mine. All of these contain the necessary ideas, techniques, and suggestions for a full life. We are re-emphasizing some of these ideas here. However, after you have read this book and some of the earlier ones, you will still have to proceed on your own to do something about the ideas embodied in the books. You are the only one who can do the job, but as you reap the rewards you will find that you are helping others as well as yourself. I often think that if each person who ever read one of Dr. Maltz's books, or one of mine, had followed through with only *one* self-healing, the world would be a far happier and healthier place in which to live.

But books alone cannot guarantee self-fulfillment. If they could guarantee this, the Bible would have changed the whole world. But it hasn't. The Sermon on the Mount would have changed the history of the planet. But it hasn't. Historians have never attempted to record the number of sermons, based on the Sermon on the Mount, that have been preached; or the number of times this portion of the Bible has been read by millions of people. Yet, reading or hearing about this great message of Jesus has not changed the world, because its teachings have stayed at the idea level; they have not moved to the practice level.

In order to have self-fulfillment, you have to practice every day. At this point I can almost hear the voices of many readers clamoring: "But I don't know how to go about it. What must I do?"

The first step is to set your goal and to believe in it. Believe, without hesitation, that you are going to reach it. What your goal is will be determined by what you want to do, who you want to be. It may be a long-range goal that you will have to travel far to reach. As you move toward it you may be reminded of an ancient proverb that says, in essence: *A thousand mile walk starts with a single step.* There may be many steps, many minor goals, on the road to your major goal. Set your sights confidently on your large objective and then start with one of the minor goals. The pathway to self-fulfillment is made easier and brighter by each attainment of a minor goal.

Suppose your major goal is happiness. You say, "I want to be happy, but I am not." Why aren't you? What steps can you take to make yourself happier? What minor goals can you reach? Let's assume that one will be the simple matter of changing your conversation. Is what you say interesting to anyone besides yourself? Decide that the next time you see Sally or Joe you will not re-hash things you've said many times before. If your problem is that you feel you haven't anything to say, read a book and talk about that. Read some interesting magazine articles and introduce what you've learned into the conversation. Have an exciting experience and share it with others.

At any rate, *stop* rationalizing your failures with trumped-up excuses, and *start* taking steps toward your goal, whatever it may be. That's the only way you can achieve self-fulfillment. And you'll be elated when you do achieve it. Self-fulfillment is the awareness of yourself as a satisfactory individual. That awareness gives you a wonderful feeling.

When you are lonely, miserable, and frustrated, you are not a satisfactory individual. You think of your lack of friends and pity yourself instead of doing something constructive about making friends. You let your thoughts linger on slights and snubs instead of asking yourself if perhaps you aren't to blame. Your entire attention is focused on what is wrong in your situation. Try turning it instead on something that is right, or on something that you can make right.

Self-fulfillment is the feeling of self-satisfaction. There is nothing wrong with that. I believe that every person who has ever accomplished anything great has had a tremendous inner sense of self-satisfaction. It is the glorious feeling of having done something well, something worthwhile.

Perhaps you are about to say, "But I haven't ever done anything that was worthwhile." Don't say it. Start thinking instead. Use the power of your mind. Go and sit in a garden; go and sit in the park. If the weather isn't good, go and sit somewhere other than the place where you live. Be stimulated by a new environment and you may come up with some valuable new ideas.

The tendency of the frustrated person is always to retreat, to crawl into a shell. That shell is usually his home. There he looks at the same four walls, the same furniture, the same refrigerator, and the same set of dishes. Such a person is desperately in need of a change, if only for ten minutes. He needs to see something new, something challenging, something that will bring to life the once-bright self-image that he has successfully buried beneath his chronic negativism. He needs to find some interest that will make him hunger and thirst after a creative way of life.

We are admonished in the Bible to "hunger and thirst after righteousness," and I'm sure this means to hunger and thirst after a creative way of life. Most spiritually alert people do have that hunger and thirst, because they haven't quenched it too often with hurts, loneliness and their own misunderstanding of themselves.

It is important to realize that every time you describe yourself or your situation in negatives, you are adding to your own self-misunderstanding, which is the exact opposite of self-fulfillment. There is no quicker way to develop self-misunderstanding than to belittle yourself, to run yourself down. We all have a tendency to do that when we are feeling depressed. You can master that tendency if you remember that *self-depreciation is destructive,* and that you will never find self-fulfillment through creating self-destructive images. You are never really as bad as your frustrated mind pictures you to be.

Try to see yourself as a perfect being. It isn't difficult.

Shut your eyes and think of yourself as being the way you want to be. If you are one of the unfortunates who is bound to say, "I don't know what I want to be," I'm tempted to tell you to stay as you are. But try again. What would you like if you were perfectly happy? Shut your eyes and try to figure that one out. Would you look as you do now? Would you dress as you are now dressed? Would you talk as you do in the usual conversation of the day. No. Probably not.

Right here I am offering you some suggestion for minor goals on your road to happiness. If you want to be self-fulfilled, how would you dress if you were self-fulfilled? Then dress that way. How would you groom yourself, wear your hair and so on, if you were happy and self-fulfilled? Change your appearance to meet your ideal. How would you talk if you were self-fulfilled? Then change your conversation to that of the new image.

When you do this the bars of your mental prison will start to shake; they will spread apart so you can begin to see your life as it really is. No creative power ever condemned you to frustration. No God, by whatever name, planned for you to be miserable. If you are miserable, you are suffering from self-created misery; and I'm willing to state that most of it is *unconsciously* self-created misery. No one decides to be miserable.

When you've worked with these simple suggestions long enough to see some improvement in your regard for yourself, start watching your negatives and don't allow the seed of any unwanted or unworthy idea to be implanted in the ground of your subconscious. Turn your negatives off by thinking their opposites. Learn to accept situations as they are without letting them bother you. Learn to say, "What difference does it make?"

Suppose you were fired from your job five years ago. So what! Probably the employer knew what he was doing, even though you say that you were one of the best employees the man ever had. Maybe that's just your alibi, your excuse. Forgive yourself and your former employer for this old hurt, and forget it.

Perhaps you were ill for a long time three years ago, and you are still mentally reliving and rebuilding that illness. If so, your negative thinking will probably cause you to be ill again.

The Bible says: "For by thy words thou shalt be justified, and by thy words thou shalt be condemned" (Matthew 12:37). Watch your words. Keep your conversation positive. You do not find self-fulfillment through self-depreciation, and you do not find it through listening to or discussing the negative thoughts and feelings of others. Nor do you find it by sitting at home and worrying. These tactics never have worked and they never will.

As we move along in this business of looking at ourselves squarely, and discovering our strengths and our weaknesses, we come to the point where we must ask, "Do I accept myself as I am, or do I reject myself?"

If you accept yourself as you are you probably rank among the minority—the fortunate, well-balanced minority. Rejection of self is a rather common human reaction, though it varies greatly in degree of severity. This rejection stems from the fact that no one is perfect, and many people who crave perfection can't face up to their own imperfections. They continually blame themselves for every mistake they make—or ever have made.

Perhaps I, too, reject myself occasionally on a minor scale. But, generally speaking, I have come to terms with myself on that point. I came to terms when I reached the understanding that no mistake I have ever made is of real importance. As Dr. Maltz says, "We are all mistake-makers, but we also are mistake-breakers." When we take the importance out of our mistakes, they become dwarfs instead of giants.

If you find that you are a self-rejector, try saying to yourself:

I accept myself today, right now, as I am. Yesterday is past. Ten years ago doesn't count. I am a human being today with a creative mind and I want to use it creatively. I have great emotions which I can use constructively. I am a today person, in a today world, and I am going to use my mind and my emotions as I should use them today. I do not reject myself. I am a rather nice human being. God created me, and if I am good enough for God, I'd better be good enough for myself. I accept myself as a valuable creative individual—individualizing life.

Add to that statement these words:
I walk this day as a dignified, creative individual.
What does that mean? It means that your posture matches your state of mind. If you walk in dignity, you feel important. Try it and see. Even the most casual observer can judge your personality and your outlook on life by watching the way you sit, the way you stand and the way you walk. The person who stands erect, walks with his shoulders back and his head held high indicates that he is unafraid; he has no fear of the future. He is a success-prone person. In contrast, the person who walks in a stooped manner, always looking down and perhaps shuffling his feet a bit, is a person who doesn't want to see the future. He has no plans for success; he actually expects to fail and he isn't surprised when he does.

I've frequently had an individual say to me, "Dr. Barker, I was finally released from my job, but I knew it was coming." That person's mind had been preoccupied with failure for years and there was nothing for him to do but fail. Of course such an individual will always say afterward. "Well, it wasn't my fault."

I'm sorry! I disagree. My mind is the center of my expereince. I cannot have an experience that my mind has not caused to happen. If I were fired tomorrow from my job as minister of the First Church of Religious Science in New York City, it would be my own fault. I'd probably tell everyone that the Board of Trustees was to blame. But I wouldn't fool myself. It would be my own fault. My mind is what I am, and my experience is the result of my use of my mind. This is not only expressed in my mind body relationship. It is expressed in every relationship I have, whether it be with people, in business or in my home.

When I go out on any occasion, the only thing I can take is my mind. The body follows along; the body is automatic. I walk into every situation with my mind, and my mind will determine what I give to that situation and what I receive from that situation.

Let's turn our thinking now to the baby Dr. Maltz mentioned—the baby coming out of the mother's womb; its first slap and first cry. That baby arrives in this world fully equipped to be a success. It arrives with the capability of *thought* and *feeling*. Then, after the necessary months, the child will add *speech*. Here he has his three great tools for living: thought, feeling, and speech. What happens during all the rest of his life will be the result of what he is doing, or has done, with his thought, feeling, and speech.

If you want to start now, using those tools in a constructive way, you may find that you are experiencing the second birth that is mentioned in the Good Book. You can change your life in any way you wish if you handle and control your thought, feeling, and speech. These three tools with which you were born are the tools, the equipment, that will take you the rest of the way.

This is a challenge. If you accept it, you can become any kind of person you want to be; the person you are five years from now will be a living example of what you did with your birthright, your total significant equipment. The individual who considers himself a miserable failure can reverse himself and become a magnificent success if he learns how to master his thought, feeling, and speech.

To repeat what I have said earlier in this chapter, it isn't easy. The frustrated person is a worrier and he has to stop worrying. He can't stop worrying until he has a real reason for doing so. That reason is a goal.

Suppose I've worried for years about my health, then I suddenly decide to make real health my goal. I start to eat sensibly, to sleep a reasonable number of hours. I take long walks and perhaps I find suitable forms of exercise. I may add other health-promoting regimes. That's fine. But unless I *think* health while I walk, eat, sleep, and work I won't reach my goal.

If health is your goal, learn to say: *"I am health."* Do this even when you are not feeling very well. Just say it.

You can even spiritualize it and say: *"God is my health."* But you still have to think it, feel it, talk it, and find routines that produce it.

You can translate this into any other area of your life. Your goal may involve a career, a happy marriage, a new home, or just a sizable bank account. Whatever it is, remember you must use thought, feeling, and speech to attain it.

I have counseled many people on the problems that come from the lack and limitation of money. While the answer to their problems is not money, but rather the awakening of the creative power within them, I start counseling them on minor goals. "Put one dollar in the savings bank today," I sometimes say. The answer usually is, "Oh, they won't open a bank account with only one dollar." I reply, "Then save a dollar a week for ten weeks and walk in and plunk it down."

This doesn't usually seem to be a satisfactory answer from the standpoint of the person with a financial problem, but from my standpoint it is a *start* on an intelligent, constructive program.

When I explain that it is a most comfortable feeling to have money in the bank, beyond current bills, the person I am counseling often looks at me and says, "I need every dollar I've got." The person who says that wants to stay in his poverty.

Of course, the dollar a week in the bank is nothing but a symbol; it is a valuable symbol to the mind. I have often said to someone in a financial-limitation problem: "Add a dollar a week to the payment of one bill, and gradually whittle it down." I say this because when your mind becomes really interested in paying bills, rather than owing bills, you will find a way to get yourself out of debt. But when your entire focus is on what you owe to this store or that concern, your attention is on owing, not paying. As long as your attention is on owing, the subconscious mind will arrange more ways for you to owe. When your attention is on paying, the subconscious mind will then begin to create means for paying.

It won't be because of manna from heaven! It will be because your mind finally is organized on a success program in the particular field of finance. Self-fulfillment will come when, step by step, you have reached the point where you owe no man.

When you have cleared one department of your life, when you have completed one of your areas of self-fulfillment, you will probably want to start on another. Always remember, whatever your direction may be, you should start with your minor goals and keep on going until you have arrived at the place where you want to go.

All of this starts, of course, with the concept that you are valuable to life. A frustrated person doesn't have this concept. It is essential to realize that you would not have been born if there weren't some reason for your birth and your life. You are not a biological mistake. The universe has too much order and plan to include mistakes. You were born to be a creative, valuable person. I believe that not a single person is born into this world who is not needed by the world. I believe that you and I are needed.

If you are a member of my congregation you may say, "Yes! You! Look at the job you are doing. Everyone needs you!" I wish it were true, because Madison Square Garden is still available for Sunday morning rental.

You can point to a Dr. Maltz; you can point to a person like myself; you can point to a noted criminal lawyer; you can point to all these people and say, "Look at them!" But that has nothing to do with it. *You* are necessary to the coordinated life on this planet or you wouldn't be here. I don't believe the Infinite Intelligence ever makes a mistake. And I do believe that you were born at the right time, in the right place, of the right parents, to do your right work.

Start thinking this way, instead of saying, "Well, I don't know. I wish I were ten years younger; I wish I'd had different parents." You didn't. Fortunately most of us like our parents, but if you don't, start believing and saying:

I was born at the right time, through the right family, and in the right location to do my right work.

This is self-acceptance; this is the acceptance of a new self-image, of a cause for being. Every living soul *needs* a cause for being.

Every living soul needs the sense of being needed, and if you have no one on earth who needs you, find somebody. I know it isn't easy. You have built up all your bars; you have put yourself into your own mental jail; you have been the judge and you sat there and condemned yourself. Now change the condemnation. Let the judge in your mind say:

I now set you free to be a creative person. You are valuable to God and to man.

Even if you don't believe it, say it anyway. And if you say it often enough and long enough, it will begin to register. You will find a situation in which you are of value. You will begin to draw people to you who will find a value in you. This is because you are now thinking, feeling, and talking in a way that makes people want to respond.

Each one of you has someone in your life who always says the same thing. When you pick up the telephone to answer and hear that voice, you know exactly what you are going to have to listen to. Why? Because that's what this person has been saying year after year. The locale changes slightly; the particular smaller events change, but the overall picture will be exactly what you heard last Tuesday when the same individual called.

Perhaps you should ask yourself, "Is that what I say over the telephone all the time? When I call someone, have I anything to say that I haven't said before?" People get tired of hearing the same thing. They know you are tired; they know you've had a hard week; they know that the work at the office has been extra heavy this season of the year—which is *all four seasons*. They know that the buses are crowded; they know that you don't like to go out at night any more. This they know. This they are aware of.

Before you make a telephone call to a friend or a loved one, *think* of what you are going to say. Judge whether it is creative, or valuable to either one of you.

Perhaps you won't say it. Or, if you are seriously trying to change your image, you will, with deliberate intent, say something different.

Your thinking, feeling and speaking make up the trinity of the creative process. With them, when they are directed correctly, you find a reason for being. Then you can literally say, "The world does need me. I am of some value to my fellow man." Then find ways of truly being of value.

Here is the situation as it commonly is found: the child is born to success; the adult grumbles, alibis, and complains that he or she is not a success. But this need not be true in your case. Change the way you handle the trinity of the creative process. This doesn't require one more degree in education; it doesn't require moving across the country to another city. It merely requires the direction of your mind, and *you* can direct your mind. If you say you can't, I am going to say you can. I have seen too many people do it to have any doubt. I have done it myself. I agree that it is not easy.

Dr. Maltz referred to "the stranger that is within you." To me, a clergyman, this means your spiritual self.

Many people today have dodged any search for their spiritual selves because past theological beliefs have been restrictive. People who claimed to be spiritual were not usually people whom others wanted to follow, or to imitate. The older theology demanded self-denial instead of encouraging self-development.

The spirit within you is not a field of repression. It is a field of expression. I am going to emphasize that: the spirit within you is not an arena of repression; it is an arena of creative expression, an expression that will produce self-satisfying benefits for you. This stranger within you loses its strangeness as you think of yourself in spiritual terms. If the word *spiritual* is a block to you, think of yourself in creative terms. Think of yourself as possibility, potential, as being a valuable human being—then the stranger loses its strangeness and becomes your habitual, normal self.

You become a creative, outgoing, healthy, happy, prosperous individual who relates to others with ease of communication when you know this self that you are. Remember that you live in an arena of expression, not of repression. It isn't what you give up that is important. It is what you do with what you have that counts.

Perhaps you will feel impelled to confess that you have some bad habits and ask if you shouldn't give them up. My answer will invariably be: "Not unless they really hurt you in some way."

I recall a person who came to me a few years ago and said that he was on the spiritual pathway. I said, "Oh, good." He said he had given up cigarette smoking. Then he had given up any use of alcoholic beverages. Then he had become a vegetarian.

I expressed my belief that this was fine for him *if* he felt such self-denial were necessary. Then he continued: "But I'm uneasy. I don't feel as though I am spiritual, and these things should have done it."

My reply was, "That's not the way to do it at all. However, I have one more suggestion. Why don't you enter a monastery?" He did not take kindly to that idea.

Of course, I have no objection to monasteries. I was merely trying to point out that he was using age-old techniques that have done more to create frustration than to conquer it. They require that you give up and go without. They declare that the Lord likes those who refrain from doing things. I was about to say that these old tenets held that the Lord likes those who are frustrated. There is not a word of truth in any such rules.

The whole spirit of God within you is seeking expression through you, and there is to be no repression. You are living in a world in which the spirit within you is saying: *Be! Become! Become! Become!*

III

The Road to Self-Respect

Maxwell Maltz

We live one life and we seek to make the most of it.

It is an imperfect life—a series of stresses and strains—but it is the only one we have.

We must take out our compass and plot our destiny. Life's highways are many and frustrating; we seek the roads leading to self-fulfillment.

And so we re-embark on our voyage of discovery, looking for ways to stand up under stress, conquer frustration, get on the right track.

It may not be easy for everybody, but most people do have hope.

First, let me quote from another letter I received from an inmate of Leavenworth:

> Just a short note to thank you for your recent visit here with us at Leavenworth. It's not often that someone, especially of your stature, from the free world, comes here to let us know that, out there, there are still those willing and anxious to accept us and love us.

He goes on to write of other things. I quote this prisoner because he writes graciously and sweetly—and anyone who can do this must still have some hope.

Even though he is a prison inmate. You—outside prison walls—chances are you have hope, too.

Now, let me quote a second letter. A man wrote it, not to me, but to a restaurant in Little Rock, Arkansas, and someone there forwarded it to me:

When I was in Little Rock the first part of this week, I noticed on two occasions, The Reader Board message at your restaurant. . . . It read: "Forgive others often—yourself never!" Each time I questioned myself of the meaning—not of the first part, but the second. The message indicated that we should never forgive ourselves, and I do not agree with this.

Inasmuch as our Lord Jesus Christ said that we should forgive our fellow man of his sins toward us, as many times as seventy times seven, we are, therefore, in agreement that we should forgive others often. However, the New Testament, in Matthew 6:15, states that if you forgive others, then your Father in Heaven will forgive the wrongs you have done. Can we not forgive ourselves if our Father can?

Secondly, Dr. Maxwell Maltz, in his book entitled *Psycho-Cybernetics,* states that true forgiveness comes only when we are able to see, and emotionally accept, that there is and was nothing for us to forgive. We should not have condemned or hated the other person, in the first pace. If there was no condemnation, there is no need for forgiveness. If we can truly forgive others, why is it not reasonable to say that we shouldn't condemn but forgive ourselves for our mistakes? It is fatal, psychologically, if we don't. Therefore, may I suggest a new copy for your Board: "Forgive others always—forgive yourself, as often."

It is a very interesting letter. For only through forgiveness can you turn your back on the frustrations of the past and learn to conquer frustration. The Fundamentalist concept that you are a sinner, from infancy on, long before you knew anything about Life, is not part of our thinking; this is not our belief. Psycho-Cybernetics means steering your mind to a productive, useful goal. It is when you steer your mind to unproductive, useless goals, that you fill yourself with frustration.

And if you cannot forgive yourself for a blunder, a heartache, a misfortune, a hurt feeling, a resentment, then you cannot clear the railroad tracks within you so that you can communicate with yourself. And, therefore, you cannot find roads to self-fulfillment—only detours.

It is a terrifying feeling to think that, in this day and age, people feel so much bigotry. Not too long ago, we heard the drums of a parade in celebration of a great man who gave up his life for an idea of freedom. It was a terrible feeling to hear these drums, in honor of Martin Luther King, Jr. and, at the same time, to know that someone hated him enough to shoot him down. So much hatred, frustration, bigotry—unrelieved, unproductive —leading to this horrible deed.

We must all overcome. We must all overcome not only personal frustrations, but our cosmic and community frustrations that have made most of us less than what we think we are. We must forgive our petty mistakes, our human errors—so that we can cleanse our souls of frustration and guilt.

Recently, when I was on the West Coast, I picked up a newspaper and read about a new weapon of the United States, an anti-sub torpedo, Mark 46–0. This article stressed the deadliness of this weapon, its vast potential in bolstering the nation's defenses. This new weapon could, it was claimed, find the deepest submarine. It could, on picking up an echo, judge it had sighted an enemy sub and take action, automatically launching its attack under orders from its brain. This new weapon was equipped with a high explosive warhead, the article concluded.

This may be splendid for our Navy, for our country, for our national security. But for us—suppose we gather in a theater of our minds, use our imagination creatively and make up our own newspaper. Here's what we write:

A lively Hunter—Man has a new anti-Frustration Torpedo: Compassion. It is his own happiness —Mark 100—it weighs nothing; it gets its tremendous zip from understanding. Its acoustic homing system can seek out the deepest running frustration hidden within us. The brain of this Mark Happiness 100 is a simple servo-mechanism within us that steers our minds to useful goals. This success-mechanism of confidence within us directs its torpedo to a subterranean target, deep, deep, very deep within our troubled minds. This torpedo, however, carries an extremely happy peacehead, removing our hidden emotional scars that seek to destroy us.

For us, this is more like it.

The Negative Warhead of Frustration Feelings

Let me tell you a story. Sometime back, I was in Costa Rica, and there were two men, both young men in the coffee business, very successful—they were partners. One, I'll call him Mr. M., was married to a beautiful young woman, a lovely, compassionate woman, who came from a family of distinction in Costa Rica. There was one trouble with him—he was suspicious, jealous. He thought his wife wasn't loyal to him, that she was carrying on an affair behind his back. And, once, when they had a charitable dance in San Jose, Costa Rica, he watched his wife waltzing with his business partner. They were smiling at each other. Suddenly, he suspected his partner was her lover.

A few evenings later, his wife wore a new print dress. She said she was going to see her mother. He wished her good luck and she left; but he was filled with suspicion. It grew dark. He walked from his home toward a huge park in town. It was a strange type of park. It was circular, with a circular area in the center where young girls walked in one direction, and a larger external circular area where the young men walked in the opposite direction. When they met each other, and got to know each other, they paired off and dated.

A huge number of chairs faced this area—under huge trees; and, from the other side of the street, Mr. M. suddenly spotted his wife's print dress. She was walking with this man, and he knew, definitely, that the man was his business partner. They sat down on a bench, their backs to him. Creeping across the street toward them, he pulled out a knife and slashed the man's face—a terrible wound. The woman, shrieking, turned around—

but it wasn't his wife at all. Neither was the man his partner. He was a well-known lawyer.

His jealously, his suspicion, his hatred not only affected him—it affected people he didn't even know. He suffered most of all, because most of the people he knew in Costa Rica disowned him.

What am I trying to say? That these terrible negative feelings of hatred and frustration—and all that go with them—are torpedo warheads that zig-zag into nothing, because these types of negative emotions hurt most the one who feels them. You create your own torpedoes that take you away from your goals when you give in to negative, frustrated feelings.

Most of us are complainers. Few of us take time off to reflect on who we are, forgetting we have the great gift of being ourselves. We use a tremendous amount of energy needlessly pursuing being less than what we really are. Negative feelings within us retard us from reaching our daily goal of self-fulfillment, sidetracking us into a dead-end of uselessness. And the well-developed ability to complain is one of them. Furthermore, when we complain, we usually believe it is someone else who has kept us from our goal.

We all know, in our own relationships with people, those who complain. I know one, a woman who is happily married, with two married sons, grandchildren— and yet she is always complaining. She's always scratching for attention, not realizing that when you scratch for attention in complaining, it is like scratching on marble —it has no effect.

We must learn to rise to our full stature of self-respect. But when you complain, you are doing the opposite—as when you gossip. For gossip, too, is a form of self-destruction. The person you hate is not there and yet you destroy him with your venemous comments.

It's the same thing with complaining. You're disgusted with yourself and you destroy yourself as you complain. You must realize this. When you complain to others, you don't lose your burden at all; it is still there.

Stop complaining! Start living!

Stop complaining! Tell yourself you're not a horrible

person; be a friend to yourself. Then you won't have to complain.

You're complaining less, but your conscience is bothering you?

All right, let's take a look at the question of conscience.

The Meaning of Conscience

Shakespeare wrote in *Hamlet:* "Conscience doth make cowards of us all." Now what did he really mean? With all due respect to Shakespeare, surely the greatest literary genius who ever lived, I don't think he knew what he really meant. And I don't think that most of the philosophers throughout the ages knew what they really meant when they talked about "conscience."

Now, let's think about this for a moment: "Conscience doth make cowards of us all." Is this statement true? Oscar Wilde believed that conscience and cowardice were the same thing. But was his belief really true? Think a moment about it. Stop reading a second—and think.

What did these two literary giants really mean when they related conscience to cowardice? I don't know—but I feel strongly that they were wrong. For *we* make cowards of our conscience. Conscience never makes cowards of us; *we* make cowards of our conscience.

It's a strange thing about life. When we're happy, when we look in the mirror and say, "Charlie, old boy! this has been a great day for me"—or, "Betsy, baby, this is my day—I love you"—we forget about our conscience. We don't know it exists. But as soon as we make a blunder, as soon as we hate someone—and we're ashamed of it—as soon as we are filled with frustration, then we think of conscience. So conscience is a negative concept.

My attitude about conscience is that it's your self-image, your opinion of yourself as you look in the mirror. And if you don't like yourself, because of some error, some blunder, some hatred, some bigotry, you refuse to blame yourself—you look for some scapegoat, as Hitler did to so many unfortunate people.

Thus, the scapegoat within you is your opinion of yourself. So you blame your opinion of yourself. Your opinion of yourself *is* your conscience, and if you make a mistake you refuse to blame yourself. So you tell yourself you can't live with your conscience. But what you really mean is: *You can't live with yourself.*

Remember this: When you fulfill yourself, when you win out in the battle of life, you're playing ball with your self-image, with your conscience. And remember this, too: *You* made the change. *You.* But when, overcome with negative feelings, you deny yourself self-fulfillment and don't like yourself, you think your conscience is bothering you. What you really mean is that you are annoyed with yourself, with your opinion of yourself—*but you can change it*.

You must become your own plastic surgeon and remove these scars of frustration that you bruised into yourself. Like me. Every day I operate in the hospital; I wear a cap, a gown, a mask. See me in the hospital. Here is the cap I wear. It's blue, you see, because many people think white is terrifying in an operating room. So, for the past ten or fifteen years, we've used blue, gray or pastel shades of green. I am a plastic surgeon: I put a mask on, a gown. I put gloves on, and now I am operating to remove a scar.

And *you,* symbolically, join me. You, too, are doing the same thing in the room of your mind. You remove your scars, your oh! so painful emotional scars.

1. When you deal rationally with threats to yourself, you refuse to let the little pin-pricks that hurt your ego cut you in two. You rise above them, removing the infection of over-sensitivity, giving yourself compassion. You cut away the scars of doubt, fear, jealousy, and suspicion.

2. You work to reconstruct a self-reliant image. You work to give to others; if you can, you will always have returns. You build your self-image not on vanity or money—but on happiness. For happiness is the only commodity in the world that multiplies by division. The more you give, the more you have. It belongs to you. Give yourself a break.

Play a game of tennis with your self-image, with your

conscience—play ball with it. If you make a mistake, blame your self-image, if it will give you pleasure; but if your self-image is looking at you, hurt that you're not blaming yourself, blame yourself, too. And you will have a fun-game that will make you laugh, and help you rise to your full stature of dignity—as a person whose goal is happiness, whose goal is a healthy self-image, whose goal has value and meaning.

3. You build within you a foundation, a scaffold of relaxation for your spirit and your emotions, to cope with these emotional pinpricks.

In Section I, I mentioned the four rules for relaxation. Let me repeat them:

1. You forgive others.
2. You forgive yourself.
3. You see yourself at your best.
4. You keep up with yourself.

How do you build? Through relaxation. And through emotional flexibility. And through a devotion to your most important task: the strengthening of your image of yourself.

You recall the confidence of the past, and you use that confidence in your present undertaking.

You use your energy for creative rather than for destructive purposes.

You live every day to the full. Each day is a whole new lifetime that will never come back; get the most out of it.

You accept your errors, and you push to rise above them.

You are on the lookout for tone—not tension.

You acquire maturity in happiness when you remember your assets: your self-acceptance, and your integrity as a *person* of worth. You have maturity in your reach for happiness when you remember your assets of self-respect and confidence.

You are a person of opportunity. You can have opportunity knock on your door from now to seventeen lifetimes and never hear it. But you must listen. *You* are opportunity! *You* are opening the door to new opportunities of improving yourself—every day.

Now, let's discuss forgiveness.

Forgiveness and Peace of Mind

You must realize that you're not only an image-maker, but an image-breaker. You must understand that forgiveness is a spiritual weapon that will help you toward peace of mind.

Peace of mind! Without it, because of frustration, you are always walking back into that little jail, that little concentration camp of your own choosing—where you create your own blackout, walking into the black tunnel of your troubled mind, refusing to walk out of it into the dawn of a new day.

Forgiveness: this is your great weapon.

When you learn to operate on yourself, removing those wrinkles from the face of your mind—that age you before your time—you then become a judge without a grudge. You are no longer the offender; you have given yourself forgiveness. When you are through with the operation, you go to the mirror and notice that these "prune wrinkles" on the face of your mind are gone. You are young again!

You have found youth—in your self-image, in your opinion of yourself, in your forgiveness of your errors. If you destroy this youth with negative feelings, you are old whether you are three or one hundred and three. But if you know how to cope with frustration, you are young whether you are three or one hundred and three. You are no longer so vulnerable to life; you are able to absorb the shocks when you take the calculated risks in living.

So now, for the first time, you realize you are not only an image-maker, but an image-breaker. You're not only a *new* image-maker, but an old image-breaker. You take off the mask; you stop playing games.

Most important, you look at a friend in your mirror: "Betsy, baby—Charlie, old boy, I refuse from this moment on to play games with you. Do you know, Charlie, old boy—do you know, Betsy, Baby—there have been some rumors about your being a conscience. But what does that mean? For you're my friend. I like you." Say this as you look at yourself in your mirror.

How about trying that when you get home today? Try it when you're alone, if you wish, so none of your family will think you've gone crazy. But try it! It's a great experience to just forget your "conscience," to make friends with yourself.

You have a moral responsibility as you look in the mirror—to forgive yourself. To forgive yourself, to shed your guilt, to come alive.

You start talking to people—because you want to. You like yourself, you're not afraid of others.

You stop criticizing yourself. You practice forgiveness. You look in the mirror and say, "I'm not going to criticize you any more. I'm wasting time; we're having a match—a tennis match. Let's play ball together." Once you stop criticizing yourself, you stop criticizing other people. You bolster your self-image, unlock your true personality.

Now, you're not ashamed to talk; you may even talk a little louder—not to shout, but to *hear* yourself talk. If you make an error, you correct it. And, most amazing, you find peace in yourself.

You let people know when you like them. This is the most rewarding thing in self-fulfillment. You've been hating everyone, fearful they're ready to knock you off. But it's just the reverse, you've been knocking yourself off.

A new sun begins to shine, through your spirit, through your eyes, when you let others know you like them. There is no shame in this; you like them and you tell them this.

What do you lose in complimenting people—*while they're alive?* Why wait until they're dead and you're putting them in a hole in the ground; you look down and say, "My! What a wonderful person she was. My! What a great guy he was," at a time when they don't even hear it?

Your Treasure

I live on top of a medical building—on the eighteenth floor. And many years ago on the eighteenth floor the people who owned the building passed away. There was a rumor many years ago that one million dollars was hidden up on the eighteenth floor. Well, the columnists wrote about it, and I decided to invite them to come have a party with me—at four o'clock in the morning —to look for the ghost who was controlling the one million dollars. Of course, no one showed up.

But, at that time of my affluence, I had a butler. He was about six feet four and had once belonged to the Hungarian Cavalry. I let him weat a splendid white coat; it made him look like a doctor. And often, during office hours, he used to stick his head way up high, as he wore this splendid white coat, and enter the room with patients, pretending he was a famous surgeon from abroad. He would then walk into another room and close the door; he would go to the mirror in a bedroom, look at himself, fix his coat to his satisfaction and march back through the waiting room—pretending he was this great surgeon.

One night—about three o'clock in the morning—I couldn't sleep, and I heard a sound on my terrace. What could it be? I wondered. It did not sound like birds; it was too loud for that. I got up to investigate. It was a moonlit night and I could see clearly. And, lo and behold, there was my butler, in his splended white coat, with pick and shovel, hacking away at my terrace apartment, at one of my rock gardens, hunting for the treasure.

I bawled him out—he could have killed me with one blow—but he looked at me sheepishly, nodded his head, and went to bed.

A month or so later . . . once more I couldn't get to sleep—it was three o'clock in the morning. So I got out of bed and tip-toed to the terrace. There was that pick and shovel. I hoisted the pick, and on impulse I began hacking away trying to find the treasure. And, suddenly, somehow, I knew someone was watching me. I turned around. There was my butler in his splendid white coat, watching me. I felt silly. I believe I blushed. I dropped the pick and marched back inside my apartment—chastened.

What am I trying to say? That we're all looking for

treasure. That we're all hungry for treasure. That we seek it out in the most unlikely places.

But, still, your greatest treasure is your dignity, your greatest treasure is your self-respect. We look at the stock market, with millions of shares traded—twelve million shares, fourteen million—up and down, up and down. But the success instincts within you, these are your blue chips; they seldom go down, they almost always go up.

Just remember that your self-acceptance, your compassion for yourself, your confidence in yourself, your respect for yourself are your blue chips. They will help you reach toward fulfilment.

How do you search for the better YOU? How do you overcome frustration?

1. You launch a new career, set out on a new voyage of discovery. When? When you give yourself another chance; when you feel you're entitled to it. When you move toward a new self-image, and learn to enrich your new self-image every day. You feed your stomach; feed your mind at the same time.

2. You realize that you must live harmoniously with your conscience, with your self-image—your best friend. Hold out your hand of friendship to it.

3. You enlist the success-mechanism within you— your confidence, your self-acceptance—to guide you to goals. You then set goals within your capabilities.

4. You visualize the better you, the realistic better you. Don't short-change yourself. You become a better person when you look in the mirror to create a better self-image. But if you don't look, you'll never find it.

5. You make your self-image ten feet tall. Your neighbors, your friends are too busy with their own problems; they're not going to make your image ten feet tall—even with flattery. You've got to do it yourself.

Your Goals in Focus

You must see your goals in focus so you know where you're going. No daydreams, no fantasies, no excursions to some island in the sun of yesterday, to a never-never land that never was. If you want to go to an island in the sun, go off-season—for eighty-five dollars. *Your goals are real.*

You must see your creative goals in focus; you must see them clearly. Even if you fail, you are a goal-striver. When you finish one goal, you start over again for another goal. If you lose, it's not fatal; you start toward another goal. You remember that even our great money-players in sports are not champions 100 percent of the time. They don't cry in their soup when they lose; the next day they're out to win. It will help you to be a champion . . . in the art of living every day . . . if you remember you'll *never* be a champion 100 percent of the time.

Leave your regrets of yesterday behind you. Forget yesterday. Live today; set your goals for today.

You must *involve* yourself with new goals—even if you've failed in previous undertakings. And, even if you have succeeded, don't kiss yourself narcissistically in the mirror. Get up the next morning and start looking for another goal.

Exercise the servo-mechanism within you to lead you toward success. We all have within us such a mechanism to steer us toward our goals—if we let it operate. Our servo-mechanism is impartial; it will steer you to failure or to success, depending on what you feed it. If you have a goal in mind and want to reach out toward it, call upon your past successes, let them glow in your imagination, and chances are that you will be successful. But, if you have no goal in mind and are instead filled with anxiety, sure that you'll fail, chances are that you will fail.

Use your servo-mechanism properly. Think of your successes, not of your failures.

Nourish your assets. They are real. I don't care who you are, you have assets. Don't be ashamed of them; be confident about them. This is not conceit—with conceit you have no goal. And, like a complainer crying out for attention, a conceited person, shouting his superiority to a world that usually does not listen, is pleading for attention, too—but has nothing.

Along with confidence—you feel humility, and you give your confidence to other, less fortunate people.

Learn to nourish your assets, your confidence, your self-respect.

And, to repeat, concentrate on today. Forget yesterday! Ignore tomorrow!

Set your goals for today—useful goals that are very dear to you. Live to the full today with your goals alive in your mind. Don't try to be Shakespeare. Don't try to be Marconi. Don't try to be Edison. Don't try to be one of the greats of this world. Remember that you're great when you're yourself.

And—surprise!—suddenly you are a great plastic surgeon; suddenly you're operating.

On yourself.

You are evolving; you are shaping; you are adjusting yourself to reality. You are creating a self-image ten feet tall. Through confidence you are creating a better you.

And then? What happens then?

You keep your accent on improvement. You feel very deeply a sense of dedication for your goals. Bolstered by your mental picture of confidence, you become involved with others and find satisfaction with others for, although you may be an island within yourself, still you belong on the mainland with other people. You share your confidence with other people. You enjoy each day to the full, each day that God gives you to live, each day so precious to us all, each day that will never, never return.

And here you are, on a new road, a splended new highway, the road which you have been seeking from the moment you opened your eyes and looked out at the world—the road to self-fulfillment.

Building a new life for yourself.

Frustration is yesterday; you have said goodbye to frustration in all its disguises.

Self-fulfillment is today.

And tomorrow.

And all the many tomorrows.

Raymond Charles Barker

During much of your life you probably have considered your conscience an accuser. Many people still believe that it is a faculty of the mind devised for the sole purpose of keeping them in line, telling them that they *should do* this and they *should not do* that. Dr. Maltz has likened your conscience to your self-image, your opinion of yourself. According to his concept, when your conscience bothers you it is because you are not making progress toward your goal, or because you do not hold yourself in high esteem.

Conscience, as I see it, is much more than a prompter telling you the difference between right and wrong, warning that you should not bridge moral gaps or cheat your fellowman. I believe that *conscience is spiritual inspiration.* It is the still, small voice that—even in the face of profound discouragement—says: "Do it. Be it. Become it."

I believe that conscience is an inner urge to get going and to keep going, not a brake that one applies in order to stop doing something, be it good or bad. Conscience speaks to each and every one of us, but some do not listen. Some fail to hear that fervent counselor within which says to the individual in doubt: "You can be. You ought to be. Why don't you be it?" To the individual who listens, the conscience becomes an invaluable guide. You cannot live in peace with yourself until you are at least making the effort *to be what you want to be.*

Conscience may only nudge you into saying: "All right. I'll try." Those words are a good sign. They are a beginner's step in your conquest of frustration. They are the signal that you are ready to break up old patterns of failure and unhappiness which you have allowed to form in your mind.

Every frustration is a conscious or an unconscious pattern of self-limitation, a pattern that tells you that *you can't* instead of that *you can*. That pattern has become firmly embedded in your subconscious and will remain there, trying to keep you from being what you can be, unless you take deliberate steps to change it. These negative patterns, habits that are hard to break, are among the roadblocks we have already discussed. They are always on the inside of you, never on the outside.

That statement may seem absurd to the person who says: "I'm frustrated in my job." Or to the one who declares: "I'm frustrated in my marriage." These are life situations. They may seem to be external, to involve only persons, places, or things in the environment. Nevertheless, these troublesome situations are actually the result of unhealthy thinking on the part of the frustrated individual.

If that person has a conscience that merely tells him right from wrong, he will probably feel guilty for a certain amount of misunderstanding and resentment on his part, but he will also be ready to heap loads of guilt on everyone else remotely connected with his frustration. Let us suppose, however, that he has the kind of conscience I have called spiritual inspiration. If he starts listening to the counselor within, the Divine Spirit, he will think as follows: "You can be a valuable employee. You can learn to understand your employer and to earn his respect. You can overlook the qualities you see in him which you dislike. Perhaps you are not always so likeable yourself."

Be assured. That inner counselor is there. Be still, listen, and be patient. If you are not accustomed to awaiting this inner guidance, you may have to be patient a while before you sense it. But when you do, its encouraging admonitions can be applied to any problem that troubles you.

The thoughts and emotions that are entertained in your mind are the things you need to face and understand. You must meet and solve every problem within yourself. There is no scapegoat. In the problem-solving process, you may have to change your views of yourself and your attitudes toward others. Quite often, you have to change your opinion of yourself, to revise your self-image. That is not always an easy thing to do.

Dr. Maltz has designated some of the people with whom he has to deal as "complainers." In my role as a professional counselor, I come into contact with such individuals, too. People rarely make appointments with me to tell me nice things. They come in with their lists of what is wrong with their friends, their relatives, their neighborhood, and the world. Occasionally, they admit that there is something wrong with themselves—but not often.

In my counseling work I do exactly what Dr. Maltz has suggested in *Psycho-Cybernetics*. I have been doing this in my own way for thirty years. I help the individual to look at himself and understand himself. I start making him realize that if he is frustrated he needs to search for the cause of his frustration within himself. The cause of frustration is never in one's job; it is not in one's marriage; nor is it in the location where a person lives.

Frustration is a *mental condition*; it is not a situation. It is a function of consciousness and consciousness alone. Therefore, the only way to cure it is to do the work in the mind that needs to be done in order to be rid of the mental block that is making you uncomfortable or driving you to desperation.

How do you do this work in the mind that needs to be done? You go right back to what we have been saying. Picture yourself as you would like to be. Count up your assets. There is not a person reading this book who hasn't some good record behind him, who does not have some commendable accomplishment. Take a moment to review your earlier years. Recall that you have done some good, some great, and some wonderful things in your life. You have been a real success in some area of your experience.

Your good, and great, and wonderful accomplishments will not be the same as mine or those of anyone else you know. You are a unique individual. Therefore, the good that you have achieved is not to be compared with the achievement of anyone else.

The good that you have done is your standard to follow. If you were once a creative person, you are still a creative person. If you were a success in one situation, you can be a success in any situation, provided you will put the same talents to work. These talents are *desire, goal,* and *enthusiasm,* an unbeatable combination.

Many persons have a lukewarm desire and a vague goal accompanied by little or no enthusiasm for doing anything about moving ahead. They have grown accustomed to the frustration of failure. They have learned to live with it. Learning to live with frustration is psychologically dangerous. A frustration is a symptom; it is a warning that a destructive habit pattern in the subconscious needs to be replaced by a constructive one.

How does one effect such a replacement? I suggest that you pay attention to your intuition, which gives you the new idea: "You can do it; you can do it, because you have done it before." Then look back at your former success or successes. Picture what they were and how you felt when you were a success. Relive this experience in your imagination. Then find the courage to succeed again, instead of giving way to a feeling of futility and the conviction that you are doomed to failure.

When you have the picture of your former success clearly in mind, take a look at your new self-image; see yourself as having completely broken the old frustration. This is important. You must see it as *having been done,* just as your mother saw a pie complete in her mind before she went into the kitchen to create it. She saw the finished creation, and then created it.

Let us assume that your frustration has to do with your job. Ask yourself these questions:

How would I be if I did not have this frustration? What would I be like? How would it be if suddenly things changed? If I were given an opportunity to be an alert, creative, valuable part of the corporation? How would I think? How would I feel? How would I react? What would I do with my flow of conversation which now is destructive? It is destructive of the company, destructive of my employer and it is also destructive of me. What would I talk about if this frustration were not in existence?

The gist of our everyday conversation always gives us away. It shows what is behind the facade. It divulges our secrets. When you say, "I met so-and-so on the street and had a delightful conversation," you are in essence saying that the person you met was not frustrated in the area you discussed. Had the person been frustrated in that area, the conversation would have been neither interesting nor vital. It probably would have been condemnatory and your remark would have been, "I met this person on the street and couldn't get away fast enough."

Your conversation discloses your self-image, your opinion of yourself. Is that opinion as high as it should be? Does it show that you are experiencing all the health, wealth, and happiness that is your birthright? I believe in a Creative Power that the world calls God. I also believe in a creative me and a creative you. I believe that all of us are vital, dynamic producers in life. We have the equipment; we have mind and emotions. This equipment is further aided by education and experience. But, in order to get where we want to go, we have to see ourselves *as being great*. We have to come to terms with ourselves on the side of greatness.

As I have stated in my book, *The Science of Successful Living*,* "Jesus could have remained a carpenter in a small village in Galilee and lived in moderate comfort all his life. Moses could have been a quiet shepherd on the plains of Media and never worried about the Hebrew slaves in Egypt. Every great man or woman on the face of the globe who has ever moved forward in the evolution of his own soul has done so because he wanted to do so, plus devising a plan for doing it. Greatness is

* *The Science of Successful Living,* Dodd, Mead & Company, New York, p. 24.

not inherited. It is fashioned out of the thought and feeling of the individual."

It would be easy for any one of us to make a list of what is wrong with life. But the important thing is to make a list of what is right. I often do it. You can do it, too. Make the list, then look at it and say:

I am a valuable part of life; I am contributing to humanity.

When your attention is on the asset-man or asset-woman that you are, on the person who has accomplished and can accomplish again, your attention is diverted from your frustrations. It is diverted from your errors of omission or commission, and you are capable of self-forgiveness for any mistakes you may have made. When your full mental and emotional energy is focused on being what you want to be, on your goal, you are not guilty of self-depreciation, which, you will recall, is self-destructive. Your mental and emotional attention has to be on the side of greatness if you are to proceed into a larger arena of experience.

Imagine what would happen on Sunday morning if I were to review some of my poor lectures just before going out on the stage of Town Hall in New York. Not all of my lectures are good; some are always better than others. What would my opinion of myself be if I did such a thing? Naturally I don't do this at all. I often, quite calmly and deliberately, stand off-stage and say: "Barker, you have done it before, and you have done it well; and you are going to do it well again." Then I walk out and deliver. I must have my mind focused in the success direction if I am going to be a success person.

This is true of me and it is also true of you. In the important arena of your life you need to review quite often the asset-person that you are. This gives you motivation. It gives you a disciplined thought-and-emotion consciousness. When you know what your assets are, and accept them as being yours, you are ready to proceed toward your goal with the self-assurance that you will reach it.

You actually have been on your way toward a goal ever since you were born, at which time your mother probably thought you were the greatest thing ever. Can't you imagine her saying: "My son—my daughter—is going to have a long, happy, prosperous, and successful life." She predicted everything good for you. I believe that, without knowing it, she was voicing the opinion of the universe. She was saying what the Infinite was saying about you: "Here is a destined individual."

We all forget, by the time we are thirty, that we are destined to our own personal greatness. We continue to forget it in later years. A little trick of mine is occasionally to walk up to a person and say, "You are wonderful." The reactions I get are amazing. Always, there is bewilderment. Always, there is that sense of "What do you mean?" "It can't be so." I say *it can be so*. Somewhere between the time of your birth and the present day you have been wonderful. Inside you there is that which is wonderful. When I jolt you, or someone else jolts you, you are encouraged to *be* wonderful.

It doesn't take much intelligence to be nasty. It takes a great deal of intelligence to live with *wisdom, balance,* and *harmony;* with cordial relationships with people and a success drive fulfilled. That takes intelligence.

"But, Dr. Barker," you may say, "I'm neurotic." That doesn't explain anything. That merely means that you have accepted a frustration as a permanent thing. If you are neurotic, take steps not to be neurotic. If books such as the ones we write help you, that's great. We will never know how many people have had neuroses knocked out of them by Dr. Maltz or Dr. Barker in the last twenty years.

Both he and I lay the facts on the line. We always say to any person in any form of counseling: "You can do it." When an individual comes back and says: "I can't," we encourage that person in other ways. We point out how to do it. Conquering a neurosis is getting rid of a self-accepted frustration that you have decided to live with in order to explain your inadequacy in meeting life.

Psychologists, and specialists in the field of psychotherapy, have ways of helping the neurotic *to adjust*. We are not helping the neurotic to adjust. We are saying to the neurotic: "You do not need to be neurotic if you will take the necessary steps not to be neurotic."

I frequently say to these self-declared neurotics, *"Do*

something different. I don't care what it is, but don't go on existing in the same old mold. Change your basic patterns in some way." If I get a real complainer I may say: "What is your favorite department store? Don't go in there for a few months. Go to another store until you have improved your thinking and moved out of your frustrating rut." Of course, this is a simple illustration of how one can change basic patterns.

I have discovered that I have to keep breaking old, set patterns all of the time. If those patterns involve past mistakes, I forgive myself for them. I don't want to be reminded of them. When memory of past mistakes does come up occasionally, I simply say: "Get out of my mind. You are an impediment to what I am doing, and I don't want you in my mind." The memories I don't want will subside, particularly if I gear my thinking to their opposites.

I have done some good and great things in my life. I say this without egotism. Rather, I have self-compassion because I know that not everything I do will be good and great. I am human just as you are. We have compassion for the sick; we have compassion for the dying; we have compassion for the poor; and we had better have it for ourselves. We had better rejoice that we can have self-compassion and self-forgiveness. This means that we see ourselves as we really are, right now, not as we may have been in the past.

The only part of the past that I wish to recall is that of my moments of triumph. These moments serve as examples of what I can do; they serve as spiritual inspiration for setting and achieving new goals. It does me no good whatsoever to review past mistakes. Let memories of them be banished from my subconscious mind forever.

At this point I would like to recommend a book called *Reality Therapy,** by Dr. William Glasser, a psychiatrist who offers a new approach to psychotherapy. He believes that there are two basic psychological needs common to all of us. These are the need to love and be

* *Reality Therapy,* Harper and Row, New York.

loved and the need to feel that we are worthwhile to ourselves and to others.

In his efforts to help emotionally disturbed people fulfill these needs he considers only the patient's present life. He states that he disregards the past, no matter how rejected or miserable the person may have felt. This is contrary to most psychiatric practice.

In essence Dr. Glasser suggests that emotional confusion is not directly connected with the past, and there is no use reviewing what happened during childhood or the growing up period. The goal he strives to help patients achieve is the ability to face the reality of their present situations and to learn to accept personal responsibility for their own experiences.

This viewpoint is, I believe, a great step forward in the psychiatric approach. For a great many years, the individual's past has been analyzed and blamed for his current problems and disturbed behavior. As a result, the past we have lived through has become our crutch; it has become our explanation of unhappiness and failure. We have relied on information about what happened in the past to furnish insight into every present problem and to aid us in finding a solution.

Let's get this straight. Your past does not necessarily condition your present. Your present is largely dependent upon what you are doing in your mind/emotion area right now. It is possible, of course, for you to point to the past and say: "I have this particular trait because of . . ." Stop a moment and think about that trait. Do you want to keep it? If you do, fine. If you do not want to keep it, it is time for you to go to work on getting rid of it.

Do you recall Napoleon's great strategy in fighting wars? It was a strategy that enabled him to make his rapid conquest of Europe. This strategy had never been used before. Its success resulted from the fact that Napoleon never hit the center of the foe's lines. He always attacked the flank. While this was a new tactic in warfare at the time, it has been used successfully ever since. We always learn from someone else's successes.

I bring this out because a person with a number of

frustrations to conquer often will say, "It's too much for me." My answer to that is take one problem at a time. Hit just one. Don't try to change everything in your life overnight, but do all that you can to overcome one negative.

This sounds relatively easy, but actually is is hard work. Don't attack the whole problem at once; don't expect to be happy, healthy, and successful all at once. Take one thing at a time and, like Napoleon, hit it on the flank.

If, through reading this book, you overcome *one* frustration, you will have profited greatly. Even though the frustration you conquer is only minor it will be a step forward. Your progress toward your goal is built on eliminating, one after another, the important negative patterns that are keeping you from being the person you want to be.

Your successful conquest of each frustration will require self-honesty. It will require self-examination and decision making. It will require new goals based on new desires, and every dtcision will need to be backed up by sincere effort and hard work.

There are people, of course, who are so frustrated that they have lost all desire to be other than frustrated. They have built their walls; they have acccptcd the fact that life has passed them by. They are in a mental prison cell seemingly without hope of ever regaining their freedom. Such persons probably wouldn't read a book like this. If they did, they would say, "It won't work." But I say, "It does work."

Once again, here is the way you wage your warfare against every frustration you have. Attack one; get rid of it. Attack another; get rid of that. You may have to keep doing this sort of thing as long as you are on this plane of life. So what! You are freeing yourself from a mental prison of your own making. You are taking down one bar at a time. Eventually all of these bars do come down and eventually you are free.

There is no virtue in unhappiness. There is no virtue in illness. There is no virtue in complaining and there is no virtue in alibis. However, there is virtue in using time-tested methods for evoking happiness, for demonstrating health, and for reaching all the worthwhile goals in your life.

It is important to remember, as you move on toward successive goals, that there are no actual finalities in life. When you issue an encyclical to yourself, a vow in which you say, "I'll never do this again," you are pronouncing a finality that is unrealistic. You are setting up a self-made law which you may have to face and negate some day.

In this connection I am reminded that as a clergyman one of my tasks is to conduct funeral services, and I have often heard a weeping spouse say that he or she will never marry again. I listen and say nothing, but I am not surprised when a large percent of these mourners return in a reasonable length of time and ask me to perform their next wedding service. Deep down underneath, the desire for happiness in the companionship of marriage was greater than the prison bars that were put up at a time of great emotion.

Again I say, there are no such things as finalities. Mind does not work that way. Mind has no fixed positions. Its operation is one of continued progress and, in the normal individual, that progress continues forever. Mind is creative and it cannot stop creating.

There are persons who will say, "I have found a new lease on life." They didn't find it; they created it. Everything in your experience is self-created. There is no creator in your experience other than you. Everything that happens in your life is the result of your use of mind and emotion. I know that as an absolute fact in my own life. Even when I don't like what I see regarding myself, I go to the mirror and say, "But *you* did it, Barker."

When I don't like what I see or experience, I know that I must refrain from complaining. Dr. Maltz has called complaining "self-gossip." I think that is a very apt term and one everyone should remember. Self-gossip is a negative discussion you carry on with yourself. You do it because you are trying to alibi yourself out of some situation. Instead of getting yourself out of something, you are getting yourself into something. You are increasing the negative mental load that you are carrying, and it is this negative mental load that impedes your progress toward your goal—nothing else. Complaints expand and make more powerful your *mental impediment load*.

Sometime, when you have the courage, sit down quietly and say:

What is my mental impediment load? What is it composed of? What, in me, is keeping me from being the individual I know I can be?

This is a form of mental and spiritual housecleaning.

Your mental impediment load probably is something that no one else is aware of. It is made up of the concepts that you have consciously or unconsciously accepted in a negative way; you have applied them strictly to yourself. As you explore and try to identify them, you will need to remember the importance of self-honesty.

Your inner wisdom is so much greater than you think it is. Your insight is far greater than you believe it to be. God equipped you with some very great equipment; it is there within you and it will work for you when you give it a chance. If you say to yourself: "Mind within me reveal what I need to know about my mental impediment," and then do some quiet, contemplative thinking, you will get your answer.

Don't give importance to the impediment that is revealed to you. Get rid of it. You do this by saying:

I now declare that the impediment in my mind has no reality, no existence, no continuity. It can never slow me down again. I now decree that it is obsolete; it has no authority. It is robbed of all emotion, and therefore it has no existence.

You will feel a weight fall from your shoulders. You will find yourself walking taller. You will do this because you have reduced to nothing a negative something that you had accepted as normal far too long.

This act of ridding yourself of a mental impediment necessitates self-honesty, self-exploration, and self-forgiveness. You begin to have less interest in what is wrong with you and more interest in what is right with you. You begin to have greater control of your experiences, the things that you manifest in your own life. This is making your outside or visible self take on the *look* of your true inside, invisible self.

We are all magnificent people when we behave ourselves, when we are creative and when we love other people. However, we don't live at the peak of our productivity and creativity as often as we should. Whether anyone can live there all of the time or not is a question that cannot be answered. But we ought to come up to the peak more often. We ought to sense the wonder of our very *being*.

The Bible says that we are "fearfully and wonderfully made." I'll take away the word fearfully. I am sure the writer of the Biblical reference was speaking of the physical body, but that isn't what I am talking about at all. I am referring to your mind and emotions—your subconscious mind. Here is the most fascinating mechanism on the face of the globe. It is a mechanism that doesn't know how to say *no* when you are saying *yes*. It is never selective.

You can pour into this subconscious mechanism anything you wish; it has no power to say *no*. Of course you can say no to yourself, and that is what many of us have been doing from time to time. We've been saying *no* and *I can't,* thereby causing our frustrations.

When you want to cure your frustrations you start saying *yes* to yourself. You affirm your own creativity. You start to self-search constructively, not destructively. You lessen your *limitation load* and you walk free.

IV

Happiness and Unhappiness

Maxwell Maltz

We have dealt at length with frustration as a way of life. We have examined its many faces, planned strategics to eliminate it from our lives so that we might proceed on the road to self-fulfillment.

In this chapter we will examine happiness and unhappiness.

Recently, I read a newspaper story about Helen Keller, who had died at the age of eighty-seven. She must have had scarlet fever, or some similar infectious disease, when she was very young; and, in early childhood, she became blind and deaf. Yet, with all her hardships, she overcame frustration, she overcame the terrible adversities she had to rise above. She couldn't see; but, nevertheless, she saw. She couldn't listen; but, nevertheless, she heard. A marvelous, remarkable woman!

Very often we don't listen; very often we don't hear. We can see and we can hear—but we cannot see or hear.

Long before Helen Keller was born, Socrates said: "Know thyself."

Long before Helen Keller was born, Marcus Aurelius said: "Be thyself."

You must learn from these oh-so-wise men. You must learn to know yourself, be yourself—and to forgive yourself.

Try to listen; try to hear. You must use your vision, too; to see in front of you, behind you, and within yourself, to remove the tumor of doubt, the obscurity of vision that constitute your frustration, your use of frustration as a way of life.

Listen! Listen to the heartbeat within you. Listen to

the great man inside of you, the great woman inside of you. Hear the voice that urges you on to self-fulfillment. It is all within your grasp. Are you blind? Are you deaf? Listen! See! Listen to the sound of happiness and the awful sound of unhappiness; we will discuss them in this chapter.

Happiness is the quest to fulfillment; unhappiness is the quest to destroy yourself. Happiness means your thoughts are pleasant most of the time; unhappiness means your thoughts are unpleasant most of the time. Happiness means you are a goal-striver, that you use your understanding and your courage to reach your goals. Unhappiness is the reverse. Happiness means you are true to yourself; you have self-respect and confidence. Unhappiness means the reverse. Happiness means you use your imagination creatively and live in relaxation. Unhappiness, once again, is the reverse. Happiness means you are creative; you grow *through* your errors. Unhappiness means the reverse. Happiness means you *never retire* from life. Unhappiness, once again, is negation; you retire in front from any challenges, any danger, any adversity.

Happiness means you are compassionate. Unhappiness means you have lost compassion for yourself, and for others. Happiness means emotional and spiritual tone—*freedom*. Unhappiness means emotional and spiritual *tension;* you lose your freedom and impose your own jail sentence upon yourself. Happiness means you are a winner in life. Unhappiness means you are a loser.

You look in the mirror. What do you see? Happiness or unhappiness? Two worlds within you: confidence—frustration. Confidence repeated until it becomes a habit means *instant* confidence. Frustration repeated and repeated becomes *instant* frustration. As long as you think and see negatively, you will be negative. In frustration you use your imagination destructively; in confidence you use your imagination constructively.

When I spoke some time back, in the Northwest—in Seattle—there was a little girl named Sylvia. She was six years of age. She rode on a bicycle, and she fell off the bicycle; and she was overcome with the fear that she would never be able to ride that bicycle again. For months she didn't. She couldn't. Then one day, her parents went shopping on a Saturday afternoon; and when they came back, there was Sylvia on a bike—riding the bicycle. And the father said: "How come, Sylvia, you're on the bike?" And she said, "Well, for two months, I was thinking how I could get on the bike; and, you know, I was thinking how I used to do it well. And, just a little while ago, Daddy, I got on the bike—and I'm doing it well."

She's six years old and yet she turned frustration into confidence by utilizing her past experience. This is an excellent example of how a person can transform unhappiness into happiness.

As a young man, I wanted to be a plastic surgeon. It is quite a while since I was a young man . . . if you believe in chronological age . . . anyway—and in those days people knew nothing about the subject. So that when I told my mother I wanted to be a plastic surgeon, she looked at me horrified.

"What kind of thing is that?" she gasped.

I said, "Well, it's a doctor who treats scars on the face as a result of accidents at home, on the highway, in industry, and children born with disfigurements."

She said, "Oh, that's a wonderful thing, Max. But tell me, how will you get your patients?"

"Mom, don't worry. I'll get my patients."

She said, "I don't know what's going to happen to this younger generation. In my time, we had much more sense than you people. What's going to become of you people? Why don't you be a little practical?"

I said, "How, Mom?"

"I tell you what you do; why don't you marry a rich girl?"

I said, "Mom, but I want to be a plastic surgeon."

She looked at me; I looked at her.

She wept—I put my arms around her.

But I stuck to my guns. I became a plastic surgeon.

I used my imagination, way back when people knew little plastic surgery; there were just a handful of men practicing it in the United States. But my imagination was constructive in that I planned to help other people.

And so I stuck to my guns; and this is imagination used constructively.

I am not trying to be conceited. I know very well that I have not always, do not always, use my imagination constructively. Nobody does; surely I do not.

But I like to draw from my personal experience when I write, and on this occasion I used my imagination in the constructive way that steers one toward happiness.

Learn from these two stories: the little girl and her bike, the young man and his profession. Learn from these stories to plan your goals and then use your imagination positively to help you toward happiness.

The Unhappiness Trap

You must keep fighting the negative forces that would trap you, that would drag you down into unhappiness.

1. You must stop the habit of complaint. That's a side of unhappiness. Stop complaining; see that you are better than you think you are.

2. You must stop thinking about your liabilities. You are only human; everyone has liabilities. Think of your assets: your courage, your compassion, your will to succeed.

3. You must stop distrusting yourself. If you don't believe in yourself, why should anyone else believe in you?

4. You must strip off your mask; throw away your colored glasses, don't believe make-believe. Be yourself, it's so much easier. The energy you waste trying to be someone else and pretending is enough to push a ship from New York to Paris.

5. You must stop ridiculing your own weaknesses. You are not perfection it is true, but who is? If you were perfect, anyway, chances are nobody would like to know you. You'd make other people feel inferior.

You must keep battling these negative forces inside you; you must keep fighting for breathing space. Don't let the forces of unhappiness trap you! You're a free man—a free woman! Don't give up our freedom!

You were once a little baby; God gave you life on this earth—not to be unhappy. Not to be unhappy!

God gave you life so you could fulfill your purpose,

so that you could affirm your individuality, so that you could assert your identity.

Not so you could fall into the quicksands of unhappiness, living centuries of frustration, endless days of misery.

Here are some more features of unhappiness—so you can try to avoid them:

1. You play games with others, with yourself.

2. You are unfriendly—to others and to yourself. You are critical of others and of yourself. You expect perfection, no one can measure up. And who would want to?

3. You act as if failure is absolutely inevitable; and, if you think in these terms, your nightmare will come true. Your pessimistic thoughts dominate your life. You color your everyday actions with: "It can't be done, it can't be done"—*and then, it can't be done.*

4. You frown all the time. Now, there is nothing wrong with frowning now and then when you're deeply absorbed in solving a problem. But if you do it a dozen times a day, you truly are carrying on an overload of mental suffering on your all-too-human shoulders.

5. You react fretfully, fearfully, all the time: "The world is coming to an end" is your theme, when it should be "It's just the beginning of fulfillment."

6. You live too much in the past: "Oh! If only I could go back to that wonderful island in the sun when I was a little child; catch the coconuts; swim in that warm, lovely water; bid servants hand me all the food I want." If this was your life, do you know you could get tired of that, too? Live in the present; make this present to yourself.

Moving Toward Happiness

Enough unhappiness? Let's try happiness. Here are some features of happiness: court them, woo them, win them.

1. You are a person of confidence; you try to be cheerful whenever this is possible.

2. You try to be friendly toward others. You're not prepared to be hurt, when you try to be a friend to

someone, and this individual doesn't respond; you realize he may be a "taker" in life, not a "giver" like you try
to be. You aim to be less critical of yourself and of others. Knowing you're human, you forgive your mistakes;
you look in the mirror and smile at yourself. You leave
your mistakes in the past and give yourself another
chance.

3. In your confidence, you act as if success is inevitable; this is the way you've got to feel. Your belief in
yourself catapults you toward success; you realize what
you can do realistically and without conceit.

4. You refuse—absolutely refuse—to let negative
feelings dominate your actions. You slough them off;
you turn your back on negative feelings; you will not
play ball with them.

5. You try to smile at least three times a day. Do
you? Maybe not, but you ought to try. When you get up
in the morning, look at yourself with friendy eyes. Don't
say to yourself: "Look at that nothing!" Do the reverse.
Say, "Listen, Charlie, old boy; listen, Betsy, Baby; I can
smile at you." Smiling is good for you. If three times a
day is too much for you or if you've having a bad day,
how about *once?* If only to remember that tomorrow
you will set a new goal.

No matter what happens, you react calmly, intelligently, as a mature person. Some days everything will go
wrong. So what? You can't be a winner all the time.
You're a champion in life if you believe in yourself, and
you will win out more than now and then.

Plato once said: "Nothing in the affairs of Man is
worth worrying too much about." How true! But if you
must worry, worry about something important. Worry
about your self-image. Build your self-image.

Four hundred years ago, in Milan, Italy, there was a
terrible plague, and thousands of people died from it.
People didn't know the cause of all this. Naturally, they
were frightened; they were terrified. Would the whole
community die? They talked about it in fearful whis-
pers; the dread of death obsessed them. And then the
Minister of Health walked the streets to see if he could
find out the cause of this plague. He had an old-fashioned ink well, with a pen, and he wrote down what he

saw; after awhile, his fingers became dirty with the ink. He walked on and, as he walked toward some of the walls of the white buildings, he wiped his hands on them. And, after the sixth time, the women looking out of the windows, the men looking out of the windows, saw him do this. Then they saw the black stains on the walls, and they thought he was the one that was spreading the plague. And so they threw him into a dungeon where he was put on the rack. So tremendous was the pain, that he confessed he was the cause of the plague —and they burned him at the stake. Not two thousand years ago! Only four hundred years ago!

Do you put yourself in your own dungeon with negative feelings? Do you *burn* the Spirit within you—at the stake—and destroy it, with hurt feelings of resentment, with tortured feelings of distress and frustration? Indeed, do you torture yourself? You die, much more quickly, when instead you should live much more thoroughly. Stop putting yourself on the rack with negative feelings, with frustrations. You put yourself in your own dungeon, so you must come out of it. Rely on the mental and spiritual resources within you. Turn to your self-image, to your good opinion of yourself.

Did you ever hear about "Typhoid Mary" who, many years ago, when we were plagued by typhoid, carried the germ of typhoid without being affected by it herself —not knowing that she served as an agent of destruction. And so the name came into being, "Typhoid Mary," standing for one who spreads a communicable disease.

Ah! but there is one great "contagion" that has great rewards, and it is a pleasure for you to spread that: and that is happiness. If you move toward happiness, if you win out in happiness, you can be the "Typhoid Marys" of happiness. You can spread it. Imagine if you could spread happiness to ten people; and then those ten people infected ten more; and it went on that way for about —well—two years. The whole world would be a better place to live in. There would be less frustration, less unhappiness, and more fulfillment. Such a simple thing! First you must achieve happiness yourself, then you can be the "Typhoid Mary" of happiness.

I know I've written this before, but I'll write it again —and not for the last time. Happiness is the one commodity that multiplies by division. Remember that! When you spread happiness, it multiplies within you. Don't be afraid to give yourself to other people. Even if they take advantage of you, remember there are other people who won't. It's not so much a question of giving yourself another chance; it's a question of giving other people another chance. Remember that!

The Happiness Habit

Happiness! Oh! what a great story. It is the greatest of all stories. Surely, God intended this story for all of us.

It's easy to get the happiness habit—just as you get into the habit of brushing your teeth. It's all up to you; truly, only you can create a happy world for yourself, no one else will do it for you. Still, this is one goal worth all your energy.

External conditions may or may not bring you happiness. You may or may *not* be happy if Sally or Mabel or Mary dies and leaves you $30,000. You may or may *not* be happy if Celia or Rose or Sarah gets rid of her rheumatism. You may or may *not* be happy if your boy gets into medical school.

There are no "ifs" to happiness. *You are happy now!* You do the best you can; you try to fulfill yourself. You don't try to help others fulfill themselves if they're not interested. Don't try to spread Psycho-Cybernetics to other people if they don't want to listen. *You* listen! *You* hear! *You* see!

Another aspect of the happiness habit—a point to remember: you dig out your buried assets. You don't let your resources die inside of you. You have resources, all of you, compassion, resilience, laughter. Ah! You learn to laugh!

Laughter! A great emotion. A feeling, a feeling. What a little humor does!

I was addressing an audience once—not too long ago —when a woman came up to me at the beginning of the talk. She said: "You wouldn't remember me, Doctor, but I read your first book over thirty years ago. And, then, I became interested in Psycho-Cybernetics, and I read your book on it. It didn't do anything for me." Now, many people have read *Psycho-Cybernetics*, and reading my book has, I know, helped many people. Still, how about this woman who said it didn't do her any good? Why didn't it? Because when she read it she thought just reading it would do her good. She didn't realize she had to be more than a passive reader—that she had to do something about things. This is not positive thinking: it is positive doing! And that's what Psycho-Cybernetics is all about. You turn a thought into a creative opportunity. You set goals, and you go after them.

You wage an aggressive war on negative feelings. You push to strengthen your self-image. You try to see yourself as you have been—in your most productive past, in your most glorious reality, in your best moments. You've had a good moment—sometime! Think of it! Recapture it—relive it! At least, try. Because, when you try, you are already on your way. You have come out of yourself, out of your prison into the world.

And, for goodness' sake, seek out activities that will make you happy. Don't force an activity on yourself just to please someone else. Some sport, some hobby that you like for the eight hours each day that are all yours. You eight hours free from the demands of work and the necessity of sleep. In eight hours you can do so many things for yourself. You're a king, you're a queen, you're a stockholder—you own stock in yourself—in your free eight hours, and the better you use them the more you will relax, the better you will sleep.

Another point to remember. Help others. It can be a glorious, rewarding experience. What have you got to lose? A little bit of your time? In helping others, you may help yourself.

Some more points for happiness.

You've got to prepare for it. This is your first generic goal that makes you alive. You also live in a climate of happiness. Avoid negative people; avoid people who are filled with negative feelings and always tell you: "It can't be done, it can't be done!" You turn around and do it. And you do it by entertaining good thoughts about yourself and others, instead of poisoning yourself with depressed thoughts about yourself and other people.

See yourself with kind eyes when you get up in the morning. Whether you scratch your back, or yawn, or bury your head in your pillow when you wake up, think of yourself with a little bit of kindness. I think you're entitled to it.

Unearth the negative feelings beneath you, be a great archeologist and dig-dig-dig: dig deep within you to uproot those evil destructive forces of negative feelings.

Every morning when you look in the mirror, start with that little smile. Try to like yourself. Try—and resolve that you will do the best you know how—under whatever circumstances—to reach your goals today. And if you fail, you fail: there's no disgrace in it and the next day you try all over again.

You must have a meeting with your self-image. You must realize that the image within you was born to greatness, to fulfillment, achievement, success. You must *prepare* to improve yourself. You must imbue yourself with courage. You must support yourself in time of stress or tension and rise above it. You must nourish yourself with the happiness-mechanism. You live happily today; not tomorrow. You encourage this state of happiness. You help others, and you help yourself. When you look in the mirror, you see a better you.

And, above and beyond all this, you must gear yourself to overcome the negative forces inside you, the forces that would drive you from that sunny land of happiness to that foggy, rain-drenched land of unhappiness.

Let's discuss this now.

Overcoming Unhappiness

First you must realize you have an unrealistic attitude when you're unhappy. You may say, "I came from the wrong side of the tracks, I was born unhappy, I never will be a success, I'm no good anyway." Nonsense! You can change—from failure to success: *you can change—*

from unhappiness to happiness. You can overcome these negative tendencies.

Who ever told you that you were born to be unhappy? No one can make you unhappy without your consent. *You* have the final say. Yours is the final judgment.

Remember that unhappiness means loneliness. No one can make you feel lonely—without your consent. What you have done—in building loneliness—you can overcome.

Unhappiness means loss of your true identity. And no one can make you lose your own identity—without your consent. You must overcome this; you must support yourself, give yourself identity.

Unhappiness means undue limitations, separation from yourself, separation from other people. You put yourself in your own jail, in your own dungeon, in your own concentration camp. No one can put you there— without your consent. You came into this world free. Why put yourself in your own dungeon of despair?

Psychologically, you must let the telephone ring. You create a tranquilizer between you and negative feelings. I am a professor of surgery in more than a dozen Latin American countries—especially in Central America . . . and it's mighty hot there . . . from eleven A.M. to three P.M. So we used to operate at six o'clock in the morning. And, during the stupefying heat of midday, most people would walk around with umbrellas to avoid sunstroke. You, too, must put a mental umbrella between you and your negative feelings to avoid a "tension stroke."

In place of an old habit of over-responding to tension, substitute a new habit of delaying your response. Let the telephone ring in your mind; let someone pick it up, they'll give you the message later—you'll give it to yourself later. You break the electric circuit of distress for a moment, so that you do not over-respond to crises, so that you can renew your energies for the joys after the sorrows that will come tomorrow. You adapt yourself, you rise above your problems.

Keep your eye on the ball—your daily productive goal—till you have reached it. How many deals in life have been destroyed during the last two minutes, the last five minutes. For years you've planned on something; you are almost there, then, in the last few minutes, you get so tired you can't see the forest from the trees. Keep your eye on your goal all the time—till you're through with it, till you reach it.

Plan to get rid of your excess tension. Think of the geyser: Old Faithful, in your mind, in the room of your mind. In the playhouse of your mind you see a sunny room. Through the window you see a geyser—letting off steam. Isn't this a symbol for you—to let go of the pressures of the day? If your imagination won't work this way, go over to the faucet. Open the faucet; then think of the water coming out under pressure. You're letting go of that steam in your mind—and you turn the faucet back.

Learn how to forgive other people—and make a habit of it. Forgiveness may bring you tremendous rewards.

I was in Spokane, Washington, not too long ago. Four couples were listening to me; they were trying to patch up their marriages. One woman said: "I forgive him, but I can't forget." But what kind of forgiveness is that? It's not easy to forgive others; when you do, you move toward fulfillment as a human being.

When you learn to forgive, you teach yourself to overcome unhappiness.

You are a unique human being in this world: God made you so. Just like fingerprints; they're never the same. You are never the same as anyone: even if you're an identical twin, you're *still different!*

Lincoln noted that God had made so many common people. No—the reverse—they are *uncommon.* No two people are the same. And it's your destiny to do the best you can. Don't imitate someone else. You mustn't do that at all.

Your self-image is your emotional and spiritual thermostat. It's your thermometer. Keep it well regulated, pulsing with enthusiasm, not with despair. Let it *tick* with excitement, not like an old grandfather's clock in a deserted room.

You look in the mirror: "What kind of a day is it

going to be, Charlie, old boy? What kind of a day is it going to be, Betsy, Baby?" Are you going to smile? Or are you going to frown?

You overcome unhappiness—fighting through your negativism—when you feel you deserve to be happy, when you think enough of yourself to put a smile on your self-image because you are pleased with yourself.

It isn't always easy. I do not underestimate the extent of life's realistic problems—I have lived too many years to do that, I must admit. When you wake up in the morning to the harsh summons of your alarm clock, I realize that it may be to face up to a day of seemingly endless demands and irritations, in which nothing seems to go right, and in which all kinds of unforeseen obstacles to your goals seem to spring up from nowhere.

Under such circumstances—and certainly such circumstances can surround you just as readily as everything going as planned—you may start off feeling a little grumpy, then begin snapping and snarling a little, and end up with a mind swarming with negative thoughts and pessimistic forebodings.

But this is the time!

Yes, this is the time when you need a friend.

John?

No.

Jim?

No.

Margaret? Joe? Helen? Doris? Pete?

No.

Yourself.

It is under such circumstances . . . it is under the painful, depressing conditions of adversity that *you* must give yourself a boost.

No one else can give it to you.

Other people may try to be helpful—or maybe they won't—but only you, in the final analysis, can truly help yourself.

In a sense, such adverse conditions are a test for you. They test your belief in yourself. They test the right you give yourself—to enjoy life, to feel happy, to win out. They test the degree of support you are able to give yourself. They test your ability to turn crises into growth situations. They test your ability to climb out of frustration and unhappiness into the warm sunshine of the happy, who love life, imperfect as it is.

Raymond Charles Barker

As you take the steps toward conquering your frustrations and reaching your goals that Dr. Maltz and I have recommended, these are important points to remember:

You are mind in action. Every experience you have is the result of the use of your mind. As mind, you are the director of your life, the ruler of your personal world. You build your own self-image and make your own decisions. You authorize your every experience by your thoughts and your emotions. Your conscious mind is the thinker; your subconscious mind is the doer. You have the power to choose, consciously or unconsciously, to be a success or a failure. It is also within your mental province to decide, consciously or unconsciously, to be happy or unhappy.

Don't be overwhelmed by these statements. I've made them before and I will make them again. They serve the purpose of making you aware of your potential, your responsibility to life. Everyone is born with a greatness-potential, but few of us achieve instant greatness. We need to learn the self-discipline that leads to right choices; to learn the process whereby we reach self-fulfillment. If this were not so, it seems obvious that everyone would immediately choose to be happy and successful and, therefore, everyone would immediately be happy and successful.

This is far from the way most individual lives unfold, and, as Dr. Maltz has emphatically stated, many people are actually on a *quest* for unhappiness rather than happiness. He likens this to a quest for self-destruction.

It is true that some people are subconsciously bent on

destroying themselves, and if they continue their negative search, they will succeed in self-destruction. In my years of counseling, I have come into contact with many unhappy people. Happy people rarely seek professional advice. Most of the chronically unhappy individuals who have sought my help have actually been on a search for ways to remain unhappy. They subconsciously found satisfaction in being unhappy and wanted to continue to be unhappy.

You will notice that I am referring to *chronically* unhappy people. A person who is experiencing only a temporary unhappiness wants to overcome it and he usually does in a reasonably short time.

Perpetual unhappiness is a result of neurosis. Persons suffering from it have seriously disturbed emotions. They do not see themselves as they are, as the cause of their own unhappiness. They blame their chronic mental state on other people, on situations that have occurred and continue to occur in their lives, on what they consider unfavorable conditions and distressing events. These are the *things* that the unhappy ones want changed. When it is suggested that what they need is a change in their own thinking, their own consciousness, they are incensed. They fail to see any need for such action.

These people are so geared to their unhappiness that it actually gives them pleasure. They love to talk about the "evils" that have befallen them. They will tell anyone who is willing to listen how mistreated they are; how unlucky, how misunderstood, and how maligned they have been all of their lives.

These self-pitying individuals don't know it but their whole basic motivation is toward failure. They are heading straight for failure via the unhappiness route. If you tell them this, they will not accept your judgment. The usual response goes something like this: "If you were in my place you'd be unhappy, too." Thank goodness I'm not in their place, nor do I ever intend to be! I am in a position where I have to be reasonably happy, because in my profession I have to give happiness to others. It is simple logic that you cannot give away something you do not have.

Dr. Maltz in his work and I in mine—undoubtedly many of you in your work—are accomplishing a great good, because we are able to give happiness. We can do this only because we have happiness in our own lives. Yet we must accept the fact that we can't give happiness to people who are not receptive, people who do not want to have happiness for themselves.

If you know an unhappy person who isn't interested in changing his thinking and developing new, creative ideas, let him dwell in his gloom and despression. Let him wallow in his "slough of despond." Remember, that is what he wants. He subconsciously desires to be unhappy. As his circle of friends grows smaller and smaller, he subconsciously experiences a perverse satisfaction because he is subconsciously attaining his negative goals of loneliness, unhappiness, and failure.

Countless unhappy people, however, do want to be helped. When one of them manifests some spark of creative interest, it indicates that he is ready to move from unhappiness to happiness.

Men and women who have spiritual understanding know that no one is hopeless, that the Spirit of God is in every human being. Those who lack such understanding will often express doubt or indicate that they are not at all interested. Most of the people with whom you have business dealings, most of the people who live near you, and perhaps most of your acquaintances are not the least bit interested in a spiritual factor in life. Most of them do not even bother to pay lip service to religious ideas any more.

This is made obvious by the fact that if all of the churches in New York City were filled to capacity at any one time, they could only accommodate ten percent of the city's population. We have no way of reckoning, but perhaps far less than ten percent of the population of New York City is happy.

The person who wishes to move from unhappiness to happiness must have an interest in the *spirit of living*. There has to be a spiritual basis for continued happiness. Perhaps you know someone who is a very happy person yet you call him irreligious because he never goes to church. I'm not talking about going to church. You

112 HAPPINESS AND UNHAPPINESS

don't have to go to church to have a spiritual premise
for living.

A happy person is dealing with a spiritual something,
whether he thinks of it in those terms or not. He is
drawing upon some inner resource that is beyond his intellect. He is drawing on an inner success attitude. Without knowing it, he is using the science of Psycho-Cybernetics and the Science of Mind, correctly. I repeat that
there is a spiritual something welling up within the person who is happy most of the time. No one is happy all
the time.

Here is an important area where mind action needs to
function. Your consciousness, and the decisions you
make in your consciousness, can stimulate the spirit
within you provided you recognize and acknowledge its
presence. Say to yourself occasionally: "The spirit within me is a sound basis for happiness." This has nothing
to do with theology. The words can be said by the Cath-
olic, the Protestant, the Jew, or the Moslem. They can
be said by the agnostic. Anyone can say: "There is
something in me that is greater than I am, and that
something wants me to be happy."

When you express yourself in this way and recognize
the truth of what you are saying, you are already on
your quest for happiness. You are seeking, and what
you seek you will find, because it has always been available to you. Everything necessary for an individual's
happiness is available. The materials needed are already
within his own mind.

Things do not make people happy. We live in a world
of fantastic inventions. Manufacturers are offering everything one's heart could desire at prices that even those
in the lower income brackets can afford. Yet unhappiness continues, and it continues among people at all income levels. Unhappy people are just as numerous in
one arena of life as in another. If you are unhappy in
New York, or in Denver, or San Francisco, you will be
just as unhappy luxuriating in the finest hotel in Miami
Beach, or basking in the sun in San Juan, Puerto Rico.

Within you, the ingredients for happiness are waiting
to be discovered. This requires mental conditioning that
must take place before the externals that we associate

with happiness appear. When you have established your inner happiness, your spiritual feelings of satisfaction and well-being, you will begin to experience warm friendships and make the social contacts you desire. You will love and be loved. You will know yourself as a worthwhile person. You will glory in your creativeness and you will prosper. The manifestations that result from happiness are automatic. They happen to a person when he is inwardly ready for them to happen.

The individual who reaches out for happiness, yet holds back because of doubt or fear, needs to take a step that I often recommend. I say to such a person: "Declare that you are happy now, even though you are not sure that you are." At such times I am often faced with a look of consternation and the reproachful statement: "That would be telling a lie." I continue by suggesting: "Well, then, tell the lie. I don't care what you call it so long as you do it." The next response usually is, "But then I wouldn't be true to myself."

Anyone who declares, "I am happy," is being true to his *real self*. The Infinite never created a single soul to be unhappy. The Divine conception of man does not include unhappiness. Unhappiness is a mental state that can be explained psychologically. For some people it may be tied in with an unfortunate situation in early years, to parents who lacked understanding or did not give love, to an unwholesome environment and so on. But these are explanations. They do not offer solutions.

In contrast, there are many individuals who were born in poverty and who had parents who didn't understand them, yet they are happy people. Why? They are happy because of attitudes they have built up in their own minds. They are happy because of what they have accomplished *within themselves* and what they have done to correctly condition themselves.

Happiness never happens by chance. Happiness is a result of sincere effort and, sometimes, achieving it involves hard work. In other instances, the happy person may have acquired happiness quite unconsciously. Such a person, undergoing any kind of psychotherapy, would show healthy basic attitudes. Fortunately, however, happy people do not need to go to psychiatrists.

Happiness is a phase of the mind that has received far too little attention. I am looking forward to the day when some well-known authority in the field of psychiatry will write a book about the happy mind or the psychology of the normal mind. Therein lies a great area for research.

We who are working in the metaphysical field know that we are correct in saying that the ingredients for happiness are within. We know that happiness is stimulated by creativity and that both happiness and creativity are necessary in the life of anyone whose major goal is success. I amplify this in my recent book, *The Power of Decision,** by saying:

"Creative thinking gives a zest to living, and you are a creative thinker when you decide to be one. The feeling that it is great to be alive is a spiritual necessity. It lessens the strains and tensions of routine functioning. It quickens new ideas in consciousness, and alerts the mind to the fascinations that are available to us. It allows no morbidity, no boredom, and no lazy thinking. It prevents us from drifting in the past. It causes us to be *today* people expecting great things in our tomorrow."

The next time you are unhappy say: "What's the value of this? What's the benefit? What do I get out of this, except misery?" I learned many years ago that there are certain things I can do without. By that I mean the negative attitudes of others and the negative attitudes in my own mind. I cannot afford to have these negatives appear in my own mind. I cannot afford to have these negatives appear in my experience, and they certainly will if I entertain them in my subconscious for long. The price is too dear for anyone who is interested in mental coin as well as in a material bank account.

It is far more important for me to watch where my mind goes than to be concerned about how I spend my money. My *mental bank account* is entirely dependent upon the thoughts and attitudes I deposit in it. Accepting my own wrong attitudes and the wrong attitudes of persons with whom I associate is as dangerous as depos-

* *The Power of Decision,* Dodd, Mead & Company, New York, p. 81.

iting worthless checks. Should I be foolish enough to deal in such bogus coin, my mental bank account soon would be depleted and my happiness would be at stake.

A wealth of right attitudes is a basic requirement for the person who is seeking to be fulfilled—seeking through self-expression to reap desired results. Place respect for your accomplishments high on the list of right attitudes.

I have great respect for my personal accomplishments in life. I believe Dr. Maltz has great respect for what he has done in his career. Both of us are fulfilled individuals. This is not because we have been lucky; it has nothing to do with our horoscopes; it is not based on our parents; and it isn't because God loves us. Everything that we have done, we have done because we wanted to do it and we have worked hard to cause our desires to materialize. We have worked hard in mind, forever guarding our thoughts and emotions, deciding where to direct our attention, seeking new ideas and pursuing new goals. We will continue, as long as we are on this plane of life, to do just that.

Look back in your own life and recall the many times when you have been fulfilled, when you have reached a desired goal and been able to say to yourself, "Well done." Count these personal blessings and rejoice in them. Then ask yourself, "What is my next goal? Where do I go from here?" Remember you are a today person who also is expecting great things in the future. There never is a time to stop, or to say, "It is finished."

Even the most discouraged person will react to an impetus that urges him on to try once more. I think Dr. Maltz gave us that impetus in his words, "Failure is never inevitable." Psychologists frequently refer to failure-prone people. We prefer to devote our attention to success-prone people.

The Infinite did not create you to fail. The motivation of the Infinite Mind that created cosmic order, that engineered the evolution of man, was not failure. Its motivation was self-expression. This is the motivation that is passed on to you and me. The great core of your needs and of my needs is self-expression. I believe that you and I were born with an automatic success pattern. It is within us. Those of us who have tapped it, explored it and brought its ideas to the surface have experienced our measures of success.

Initially you are a success person, not because you want to be, but because you are. When you discover that you want to be a success person the doors to the treasurehouse of ideas that are within you will open. Try it and see. Everyone wants to be a success. This is intuitive.

Many failure-prone people have changed to success-prone people. You can do it, too, if your present pattern is one of failure. Realize that you were born to succeed. I know that whatever caused me to be born, created me to succeed, equipped me to succeed, and expects me to succeed. Therefore I had better succeed.

The way to start succeeding is to declare that you are successful. At this point we are faced, once again, with those certain someones who will say, "But I am not successful." Perhaps you are not successful career-wise. You may, however, be a success at boiling water, or a success at cooking a hamburger. It is important to note your areas of success. Everyone has them. Even the most defeated soul can probably fry two eggs.

Success motivation is a spiritual motivation. It, like everything else, has a creative cause and responds when recognized—just as you and I do.

You walk down the street and hear someone call, "Hey! Wait a minute, Al, I want to see you." You turn around, see an old friend and are pleased that he recognized you. Something of this sort happened to me not long ago. I was shopping in one of our large department stores when someone called my name. As I looked up, there, standing only a few feet away, was a man I hadn't seen for several years. We had a pleasant chat and I was pleased to be recognized by the friend who had called my name. But had he not called, I would have never known he was there. I would have had no one to respond to.

Similarly, your success motivation has no one to respond to unless you recognize that it is there in your mind and ready to be called into action. You are the one who must do the calling, just as it was necessary for my unseen friend to call me.

By the way, I told him that he looked wonderful and he was pleased. Actually, he didn't look wonderful. He shouldn't have been wearing such sloppy clothes, and this brings up a matter of considerable importance. When people look at you, what do they see? Do they see a happy person? Do they see a person in quest of happiness? Do they see a success-prone person? Study the people around you when you ride on a bus, walk through the park or drop into the corner drugstore for a soda. See if you can pick out the ones who might as well be waring a label marked success.

Now look at yourself. Do you look like a success person? Does the word happiness shine out in your personal appearance? If it doesn't you had better start changing. In our wonderful modern age this is quite simple, and it isn't even very expensive. You can always change the outside of you because it is only a facade, but I am advising you to change the outside to match the inside of you, provided the inside is vibrant with the spirit of living.

Look like a success person. The cost will never be too great, and changing your appearance need not necessarily be tied in with modern styles.

Wonderful Queen Mary of England, during the last twenty years of her life, wore the most outdated clothes anyone could have worn. But she looked like a success person. You knew exactly who she was, and you knew that she was born to her station. She wore skirts down to the ankles; she wore those interesting hats, and she always carried an umbrella even on the brightest days. She was out of fashion and it didn't bother her a bit. She had been Queen of England, and in her mind she still was, even though she had witnessed the reign of two of her sons and, later, her granddaughter. You looked at her with her erect carriage, her definite walk, and you knew you were looking at a success person.

You will find that dressing the part makes it easier to play your success role. Start tomorrow morning. You are no longer living in an era where you keep good clothes for Sunday. You need to look as much like a success at ten o'clock on Monday morning as you do at eleven on Sunday.

I am not sure what people see when they look at me. I am a person who is in the public eye almost all of the time. Some of my public may not like what they see. They may even chide me for being overweight. According to the science of Psycho-Cybernetics, I should put a pattern into my subconscious mind that would go something like this: "I am very tall, very thin and very handsome." If I made this my constant affirmation, my subconscious mind should become convinced and get busy on the job of making me very tall, very thin and very handsome.

The question is, would this make me any happier, and if it did what effect would that have on my friends? Are your friends and your loved ones better people because you have lived among them? Or, when you look in the mirror do you say, "I think I'm quite a nuisance to everyone." Do some thinking on that. Are people better because they know you? I'm not talking about finances. I'm not talking about your Christmas-gift list. I am talking about *that which you are,* and that which you radiate.

When you have answered that question to your satisfaction, here is another check you might make. Is your social life as active today as it was ten years ago? If it isn't, don't kid yourself. Something is wrong with you. Don't offer the excuse that everyone you know has left town. Think of all the people who have moved in since these friends went away. Don't use the alibi that your husband has died and no one wants single widows at a "couples" party. This may be true, but find some other widows and have a grand old time. The excuses for loneliness that I listen to are so numerous that, if laid end to end, they would reach from here to Chicago.

Unhappiness and loneliness are curable. If you are not invited out as much as you were ten years ago, get going. Do something about it. On occasion, I have asked some unhappy individual, "Do you know three people whom you could call and invite to lunch? Not all at once, perhaps just one at a time?" I've been shocked and distressed when the answer has been "No." That is serious business. It means that something needs to be done.

I know of one person in particular who has made a complete about face. She has stepped out of her loneliness and become a moving, social person. She is sought after because people *feel better* after associating with her. What did she do? She worked in her own mind to change her attitudes. She started to devote her attention to happiness and direct it away from feeling sorry for herself. She began to take a creative interest in herself and in others. She isn't a "preachy" type—far from it —but today the highest compliment paid her by those who know her is, "She inspires."

In order to be a success you have to talk and act as if you were. One of the axioms of my own teaching is: "Act as though it were so, and it will become so."

Be positive in what you say, but don't be ridiculous. I make that statement because I am reminded of one of my instructors when I attended school in a distant town. He met me at the train one day. To my greeting of "How are you?" he gave this instant reply: "I never felt better and I never had more. But I expect to feel still better, and to have still more. I am spiritually perfect, morally okay, mentally alert, and financially improving." The man was an unmitigated bore, as you can well realize, and he always gave this stock reply whenever anyone inquired after his well-being.

I am certainly not asking you to follow my instructor's example. Just put a feeling of happiness, a feeling of success, into whatever you say. And for goodness' sake vary the format.

Back in the days when I was a youngster, we used to have a family reunion once a year. One of our distant cousins had a son who, some folks said, "wasn't too bright"; I suppose the modern word would be "retarded." When I was fourteen, this distant relative must have been twenty-five, but his intellect hadn't developed along with his chronological age. Each year he would come to my father, who was a middle-income man, and say, "Hey, Cousin George, how are you doing? How much money do you make?" My father, looking very serious, would reply, "There are a few days when I don't make $1,000." The young man would blink in astonishment and then go around telling all of the other relatives, "You know George is rich. There's a few days he doesn't make $1,000." Luckily all of the older members of the group knew our circumstances. We had a very comfortable, middle-class home.

I am sure my father projected his own degree of prosperity, success, and happiness just as I am advising you to do. He had what Dr. Maltz has described as human dignity.

Dignity is a quality of utmost importance to each of us. Don't mistake it for the act of behaving politely. Politeness has nothing to do with it. I'm not speaking of a dignity that has a stiff-necked, overly pompous quality; a false dignity that might be used in an effort to impress someone. I don't want to impress others. I only want to impress myself with my own integrity and my own worth. I am the only person I will have to live with, I believe, throughout millions of years.

Each individual lives unto himself alone. This is true whether a person is married or not married. It is true whether you have loved ones or do not have loved ones. It is true whether you do or do not have friends. In the last analysis, each one of us lives life alone. Because this is true, I want my dignity for myself alone.

The human dignity that Dr. Maltz and I speak of is a matter of self-acceptance. For me, it is a matter of knowing who and what I am. We are back to that question the importance of which I so often stress: "Do I like myself?" When I ask that question, I always reply: "Yes, I like myself." This is not a matter of human ego, though I have that, too. Every successful person must have it. Never decry your human ego. Use it!

When someone tells you that successful people usually are apologetic about their success, don't you believe it. Similarly, when you are told to be "as meek as Moses," go back and read the story again. See if you can find one instance in the life of Moses when he was meek. When you are told, "You ought to be like Jesus," think of the man. There was nothing meek about Jesus. A man who can say, "I am the Light of the World" isn't apologizing for life. Here was a man who had accepted himself. He was a man who knew who and what he was. The *who,* in our cases today, is what we have made of ourselves. The *what* is the original self with which each of us started.

Suppose you want human dignity, but believe that you haven't made of yourself what you want to be. It's not too late. It's never too late. Start now to make yourself loved, to make yourself worthwhile. Making this effort, and building up a satisfactory self-image, are responsibilities you cannot dodge and still be successful and happy.

Dr. Maltz and I have arrived at an overall self-acceptance, I believe. Yet we make our mistakes now and then. But we don't wallow in them. We know where we are going and we know that we must be on our way. There is no time to look back at the past and regret anything that has happened. We are today people, looking forward to tomorrow. We are both in professions that we wanted to be in.

If you are in a profession or a job you don't want to be in, get out. Quit. Then get into something you do like. You will have to take the same steps we have taken. We have worked on inner attitudes. We have worked on some of our fears. We have worked to overcome anger when we have been incensed with some people. And don't think we haven't been actually livid now and then.

The point I want to make is that everyone needs to aim for the human dignity that is one of man's most prized possessions. If you don't have it, you can go after it. It is not beyond your reach.

The thing to remember is *you can do it.* Also, if you don't have the urge, the desire within you, you can *not* do it. It is up to you, and it is up to me, to be and become what we want to be.

V

Winning Out over Crises

Maxwell Maltz

In conquering frustration, we must learn to deal with crises that bedevil us. For much of life is crises and problems; we cannot run away from challenge.

We must learn how to change crises into opportunities for growth. This is quite a trick but it can be done. And, in so doing, we conquer frustration.

We must say this: that any man's hope and self-respect are our hope and self-respect, because we are all involved in the glorious adventure of self-fulfillment. Any man's death diminishes me.

There was a death, by violence, of a great man, Senator Robert Kennedy. Thousands and thousands of people stood outside St. Patrick's Cathedral in New York City—watching thousands and thousands of people enter the church to pay their respects to Robert Kennedy. And thousands upon thousands, probably over a million, all the way from nowhere to nowhere; from New York to Washington, from nowhere to somewhere untold thousands of people watched a train bring his body to its last resting place.

I wondered as I watched the people going into the church, wondered if they really understood—wondered if they really went to pay their respects to a free, great individual who had died in violence; or whether they were paying homage to the rebirth of their own sense of self-respect—their own sense of dignity. I believe they paid respect. The millions of people, as they waved at the train, were not saying goodbye to a man who had passed away in violence; they were saying hello to a man's dignity that will remain alive forever.

More than that, they were saying hello to their own dignity. It was through the violence and death of one man that they suddenly realized that they, too, had greatness within them. For there *is* greatness within every one of us. We must resolve to see this.

Too often, we resort to violence on ourselves—to violence on our own dignity, because of frustration, which brings with it resentment and hatred, brings with it the fact that we are traitors to ourselves. And, symbolically, we put a knife in ourselves, committing violence upon ourselves because of some error, some blunder, some heartache. This is the beginning of the discord— the riot within—and, to repeat what I wrote earlier, no amount of policing of the world can ever bring peace in this world unless we learn to police ourselves; unless we learn to quell the riot, the hatred, the resentment within our own hearts.

We must know that we can never be friends to other people—regardless of race, color, or creed . . . unless, whoever we are, we have two things in common: dignity and self-respect. And I like to feel that Senator Kennedy lived to show us that.

We learn to fulfill ourselves, to bring that peace of mind that we are all searching for, by learning the terrible violence we spend upon ourselves—even though passively—through this terrible burden of frustration. Now, we all have frustrations, of course—frustrations of every day—but I'm not writing about that. I refer to the chronic frustrations with which we obsess ourselves day in and day out, reliving past misfortunes, errors, old hurt feelings—not realizing they no longer live, for they are the past.

Now how do we overcome these chronic frustrations? How do we survive crises and leapfrog forward in spite of them, turning them into opportunities for growth?

Well, we must repeat: The example of Senator Kennedy should be a reminder for all of us that, through compassion and self-respect, we can learn to overcome frustration; through compassion and self-respect we can learn to move through crisis to new life.

Your enemy within you is the conscience, the image of years which causes you to shrink to the size of a microbe. You overcome this enemy by encouraging the operation of your success-mechanism. We will discuss this in our final chapter.

But it is *you* who turn external chaos into constructive living. It is *you* who make a crisis a dynamic opportunity for growth.

Your "Wonderful Computer"

Not too long ago I read a newspaper story about a computer that could diagnose illnesses. Information on the principal diseases and their symptoms is stored in a memory device. The physician feeds a patient's symptoms into the computer, which tries to match them with those of a particular malady.

The system uses a photographic master film as the memory device. The symptoms of each disease are recorded in transparent lines varying according to the significance of each symptom for that illness.

Fascinating, indeed; but now let me tell you of a far greater electric computer within you. Within all of us, hidden right in the mid-brain, an electronic computer—no larger than the size of a small hazel nut—something that no scientist, or all the scientists of the world put together, could ever develop. A computer that you, alone, and no one else, uses to diagnose—not to your disease, but your health. Because Psycho-Cybernetics is mental health. Psycho-Cybernetics teaches you to fulfill yourself, to rise above crises and to find in them opportunities for self-realization.

This is your "wonderful computer."

Now, if you can reactivate the success-mechanism within you, the success instincts within you, you will be able to overcome frustration.

To repeat, here are the seven key characteristics of frustration:

1. *Fear*. With a goal in mind, you can change fear into an opportunity for growth.

2. *Aggressiveness*. You step on other people's toes to gain what you think is fulfillment, but it produces emptiness, for whenever you hurt someone else, you hurt yourself twice as much.

3. *Insecurity*. No one can make you insecure, without your consent.

4. *Loneliness*. No one can make you lonely, without your consent.

5. *Uncertainty*. When you reach for a goal, you bend uncertainty to your will.

6. *Resentment*. The twitch of the tensions, the gout of the mind, the daily cancer within us that robs us of our sense of fulfillment, bringing termites to live within us, boring holes in our mind and our spirit, leaving us empty as human beings.

7. *Emptiness*. Symbolically, we take our integrity, our self-respect, our self-image, and we put them in a valise; we then go to an airport, put the valise in a locker; we lock the locker—and throw away the key.

Turn your back on these qualities you may find in yourself. Purge your system of their poison.

God gave you more than this—much more. He brought you into the world with a purpose.

You are born to seek and achieve fulfillment; and you can not and dare not stand in the way of that fulfillment, even though you are sidetracked by some negative feeling, derailed by a mistake, crippled by a heartache or guilt, or some other corrosion of your spirit.

You must remember that, in the room of your mind, you should set up a decompression chamber where, when you are overcome with frustration, you can get back to yourself, reassert your identity, regroup your positive instincts, giving yourself that other chance that every human being is entitled to.

At a lecture, some time ago, I spoke on the mental and spiritual potential of man. It was on a Sunday afternoon: there were a number of people on ths dais—psychiatrists, a rabbi, a minister, a priest. And there was some secretary who was continually answering the telephone that kept ringing. It annoyed me and, when I got up to speak and the phone rang, I took the receiver off the hook; there was no more ringing.

That should be a symbol to you: under pressure, let the telephone ring; don't make a mountain out of a molehill. You become self-reliant, overcoming this little problem, surmounting this small aggravation which, if you wanted, could become a major aggravation.

Learn to relax so that you can solve problems, dissolve crises. So simple, yet so difficult to achieve. Relaxation, denied sometimes even to millionaires and kings —you cannot buy it.

The Search for Peace

The world is longing for peace—peace of mind. It longs for an end to violence, to suden death, to the explosiveness of frustrated people. It longs for people who can stand up to stress calmly and with self-respect—and then alienated, violent people destroy them. So many unnecessary deaths! We must seek peace from within, seek it with all our hearts.

We must find peace—inner peace—even in crises. Even in times of trouble.

Marcus Aurelius said:

"Be like the promontory, against which the waves break, but it stands firm, and tames the fury of the water around it."

This is what we all must be in times of stress.

In Genesis, there is a phrase (13:8): "Let there be no strife, I pray thee, between me and thee . . . ; for we be brethren."

Let's change this: "Let there be no strife between you and your self-image—that great, great person within you; because you are one, an image, in God's Image."

You must learn to overcome your fears, to live with them—in crisis and in calm. Anxiety, to repeat, is a form of fear and may be useful and creative—if your imagination is creative, and if you have a goal in view. Perhaps you are fearful of not achieving your goal. But, if you have a goal, you must try, you must get your feet wet before you can swim. If there are a dozen different ways to reach that goal, you must choose *one* way to achieve it—you can't reach it the dozen ways at once. If you fail, you start again; and, your failure does not stop you, for there are many other goals in life for you. All of us are goal-strivers; if we fail in one goal, we try again the next day for another. We don't give up.

Back to fear. I took off a little to the side of my subject here, so let me make my point about fear.

To illustrate, let me tell you a story:

Many years ago, I went to Santo Domingo. The dictator Trujillo was alive. I went there to operate on the daughter of a general who had been in an auto accident. Her face was disfigured.

The First Lady of the land knew I was to operate on this child; she insisted on watching the operation.

I thought it would be too difficult for her to watch and I went to see El Jefe (the Chief) at the Palace.

I said: "The First Lady wants to watch the operation."

He said: "Let her! If she wants to watch the operation—if she faints—that's her hard luck."

Well—I had an American passport, I was nineteen hundred miles away from New York—I wouldn't think of arguing with the dictator: I wanted to go back to New York. So I did not argue with him. I knew the First Lady would insist on witnessing this operation. I selected my operating staff. I chose two tall doctors as my associates and spoke to them in Spanish, and I said: "You two will stand on either side of the First Lady and, if she turns pale and seems about to faint, I'll nod my head and you whisk her right into an adjoining room."

They were alarmed at this—they didn't want to touch the First Lady—but I said, "Don't worry, I got the O.K. from El Jefe."

I operated. They stood in caps and gowns and masks, in the operating room, alongside the First Lady—who was attired the same way. The general of the Army, the father of the patient, was also attired in operating room cap, gown and mask. This covered his military uniform; I knew he had a gun in his hip pocket.

Nevertheless, I operated—then, suddenly, I heard a "plop!" I turned around, expecting to see the First Lady—but it was one of the surgeons who had fainted. The First Lady helped to pick him up and get him into an adjoining room; then she returned to witness the rest of the operation.

Funny—yes; but sad. Every comedy has tragedy in it. Every laugh has a tear to it. He was a man whom I had trained for many years. He was a great surgeon—yet look what fear did to him. He fainted—out of fear. How terrifying it is to lose all your dignity—because of fear.

My point about fear is this—and I believe my story illustrates it: To have peace of mind you must conquer fear, and fear breeds in your imagination. It will, anyway, if you let it. The most terrifying misfortunes, which you think you can not endure, will probably never even happen. This surgeon—who fainted—was aware of the realities of the operation; he did not fear them. Some unrealistic fear took root in his imagination, and he could not conquer this fear.

You conquer fear through a process of inner strengthening. You conquer fear through building your self-image, through accepting your fears, through acknowledging your frailties, through believing in yourself no matter what happens.

When you reduce your fear, automatically you increase your peace of mind.

Avoid aggressiveness of the wrong kind. And avoid aggressors of the wrong kind . . . the takers in life, the revengers in life, life's violent people, the people who grab and complain and take—never, never, never in a million years, being able to achieve fulfillment as human beings. For they are the real robbers of the world. What? They don't rob from you? But they rob themselves—of their own integrity as human beings.

Aggressiveness has validity—if you have goals. Aggressiveness can go with a confident belief in yourself. But aggressiveness doesn't mean stepping on people, throwing your weight around indiscriminately.

The creatively aggressive person does not hurt others; he improves himself—even if he fails—because he'll give himself another chance.

When you learn to properly channel your aggressiveness, you move out toward erasing your frustrations, feeling inner peace.

You realize that you are not inferior. In the satisfaction you feel from healthy aggression, you feel better about yourself. You are a child of God, capable of blundering but capable of rising above it. And, in your dynamics, in your freed, healthy, social aggression, you move toward goals and feel successful. You feel more self-respect, you eliminate hate. You do not hate yourself; you do not hate others.

You feel at peace with yourself.

In spite of uncertainty.

In spite of failure.

Your life will always be uncertainty; it will always have some failures. No matter who you are. This is unavoidable—it is an element of the human condition.

At the turn of the century, there was a man named Paul Ehrlich, a great Viennese scientist. In Vienna they suffered from the terrible scourge of syphilis, that greatly feared social disease of those days. But they knew of no kind of miracle drug, like Penicillin, to cure this dread social disease. And so it was Paul Ehrlich's job to discover a medicine to cure this terrible illness.

Day in and day out he worked on it, year in and year out. And, finally, he discovered the cause—and the cure. He called the cure "606"—because he *failed* 605 times in eleven years! Read this last sentence again; let it sink in. Now don't you keep complaining that life has been unkind to you because you failed to reach some little goal, once or twice.

I don't ask you to be a Marconi. I don't ask you to be an Edison. I don't ask you to be a Paul Ehrlich. I ask you to be something greater than that. I ask you to be— *yourself*. Who is the greatest human being in the twentieth century? You! You are—to yourself. You must feel this way about yourself. Not egotistically. Not narcissistically. But with an appreciation of your need for self-interest, with an appreciation of your need to give to yourself, with an appreciation that you are trying to make yourself a bigger person—and no one can do better than that.

And remember this: If you have inner peace, that little contribution you make—of peace of mind, of making yourself respected, of dignity—makes you ten feet tall. It is a community affair; it's—communicable. You can spread your health. If you spread that health of self-respect to ten people, and they spread it to ten others— *you* are the greatest person of the twentieth century.

Because, in your own little way, you will stop the violence that caused the death of Senator Kennedy, that caused the burial at night, in the darkness, of a great man. But—*his* self-respect is there. I can hear him talk to all of us: Live in it; grow in it; expand in it. This is far greater than all the politics, than all the wars, than all the riots. The millions of people, simple—not rich or poor—people who make up this universe, were watching, saying farewell to a man, yet saying hello to their dignity.

We must all try to stop the flow of resentment that robs us of our emotional and spiritual security. Resentment: the twitch of tension, the gout of the mind, the cancer within us that robs us of our self-respect.

One more story. About a man who worked in an insurance company, who hated his boss who didn't give him a raise in pay. He was filled with hatred; he'd get to his office five minutes to nine o'clock, and you'd think he came early to be a world-beater that day. But, on the job, he sat and hated, hated his boss for not giving him his raise.

Five minutes to five, time to go home. He arrived home, still overcome with his resentment. At the dinner table, his little girl of seven spilled her milk on the table. Without thinking, he slapped her.

Then—he felt horrified. He loved his little girl. He couldn't sleep that night; he ran out of the house to go to work. Five minutes to nine, he sat down, looked at his watch. He began to hate his boss.

"What am I doing to myself?" he wondered en route home. "I'm ashamed to go home." He couldn't face his little girl; he had slapped her. But he had to go home. He got off the bus. And, suddenly, out of the doorway, his little girl came running to him; he lifted her up, she kissed him, he kissed her. Then he brought her back to the ground. He cried.

He said: "But, I slapped you last night."

She said: "Oh! Daddy! That was a million years ago."

Remember this story. For, if a child can overcome resentment, can overcome the result of these small violences that destroy people, you can learn from this child.

Through forgiveness, she forgot her hurt, buried it in the past.

Your hurt feelings, your failures are of another world —they are a million years ago. Your resentment— which will hurt you more than anyone else—the chances are that you are feeling this resentment against someone who doesn't even know you're alive.

Bury your resentment; find goals and live. Stop being a zombie. Stop walking around like a somnambulist—a dream walker—in a world of reality, unable to adjust to it. You are a sleepwalker, you've hypnotized yourself with negative feelings. Wake up to a new life!

In this chapter we have discussed violence and the healthy way to use aggression, and avenues leading to inner peace. We've discussed crisis situations—for we must learn to rise above crises, to grow through crises.

Now I'd like to give you a first aid kit. A first aid kit to turn a crisis into a golden, enriching opportunity:

1. *You let the telephone in your mind ring.* Make believe you're so loaded with money that you can have five people pick up the phone for you. You're letting the telephone ring: you're not picking it up. This gives you a tranquilizer—a buffer—between you and your negative feelings. You insist on your relaxation, you protect yourself from negative feelings. *You stop over-responding to crises.* You substitute a new habit of delaying your response for an old habit of over-responding. If you don't feel emotionally rich, all you have to do is take the receiver off the hook.

2. *You deal with crises with reason, not with worry.* Relax. Relaxation is Nature's greatest tranquilizer. See yourself at your best in crises. Keep up with yourself in crises. But stop worrying; worry will only hurt you.

3. *You make relaxation a habit.* You work to make relaxation a habit and a goal in itself, repeated and repeated, like the habit of brushing your teeth, until it becomes second nature. Eventually you have *instant* relaxation. When you need it, in times of stress, you have it. You can call upon it whenever you want to; you can train yourself to it.

4. *You keep your eye on the ball.* By this I mean you keep your eye on your daily goals. Keep your eye on the

ball; never lose sight of your goals. Don't let crises turn you from them.

5. *You keep your self-image well oiled.* You keep it well regulated. You work on ways to strengthen it. Most people spend a lot of money and effort on their cars, and then they have to keep changing them. You invest your resources in your self-image. You're smarter. You keep your self-image well oiled—with a little bit of compassion. This costs you nothing. You are richer for it. You increase your investment in yourself—and you will never trade yourself in.

How do you turn an aggravating crisis into a golden opportunity? How do you survive stress? You have your first aid kit. Here's some more to help you.

1. You practice without pressure. You prepare for crises in your mind—when you're alone—you think about how to act.

2. You react aggressively and creatively to a crisis by recalling the confidence of your past successes.

"But, I never had *any* success in my life. What are you talking to me about—recalling my past successes?"

But we have all had successes. No matter how many failures. If you hear a record that's old, and you repeat it and repeat it, what do you do for inner peace? If you can't stand the gaff . . . the noise . . . you change the record. Yes, you can change your own record. If you have within your mind the repetition of frustration, and the record begins to pall on you, you put another record on in its place. You substitute a record of happiness and of confidence. You recall the days of your childhood, the moments of pleasure: in the sun, a flowing brook, the chirping birds. Or, if you lived in the north, skiing down the slopes. You did something right sometime. You were happy once in a while anyway. Remember these pleasant moments; make a new record of them. That is the beginning of a goal for now.

3. You stop making mountains out of molehills. We all have troubles and problems all the time. Don't make them any worse than they are.

4. You keep your goals in mind at all times. Don't let stress block your view. You have goals in view, and you know you'll get there, no matter what it takes. You've

got to fight for your rights, for your human dignity—to reach it and realize yourself.

5. You take your chances in life. You may make mistakes—even in crises. You are a mistake-maker, but you are also a mistake-breaker—and you tell yourself you will survive.

6. You shadowbox for stability like the great prize fighters of the past. Jim Corbett, who won the championship over John L. Sullivan, once said that long before the contest he practiced shadowboxing before the mirror —ten thousand times before the bout. You don't have to practice ten thousand times, but now and then it will help you. When you get up in the morning, you go over to the mirror and you shadowbox. Ah-ha! You gave frustration a knockout blow. Well, it sounds ridiculous; so you laugh. But even this little exercise is good for you. It's good to be able to laugh at yourself. If you learn to laugh at yourself, you can laugh at your frustration, too. Don't take your frustration too seriously; don't take crises too seriously.

7. You refuse to fear crises. You stop telling yourself you're unfortunate. Every crisis should be an opportunity. It's a signal for you. Make it work for you, instead of against you.

When Babe Ruth struck out, reporters would ask him what he thought about on striking out.

And Babe Ruth said that he thought about hitting home runs.

Remember this. You don't remember the times—the thousands of times—that you struck out. You remember your home runs. You see them soaring 450 feet into space. You are a winner. You are—in some way—a Babe Ruth. In some way you're a champion.

Let me tell you another story. In San Diego, there was a minister's son—I was speaking at a church there.

He said to me, "I have been trying to play the guitar, and sing, and I get all mixed up, and it doesn't work together."

I said to him: "Well, isn't there some record of someone you like, who can play and sing the song together?"

"Yes, I'm trying to be like him."

"Well, this is the error you're making. Listen to him

play and sing at the same time; but don't try to be him —try to be yourself. Learn his technique—how he does it—and substitute yourself on your own record."

A month later I came back, and he had learned, by the technique, how to sing and play at the same time. And he did it very well. He had a goal of himself in view—not someone else to imitate.

Another story. When I was in Texas, there was a woman who honored me greatly by throwing bouquets at me about Psycho-Cybernetics—how much it had meant to her. I thanked her.

She said: "I used it on my son. He is a high school student, and he's trying to be a discus thrower; and he was terrible. He was unhappy that he couldn't be better. I gave him the book to read, and he was only seventeen. A month later, he did it so well; and then, finally, they had the contests of all the Texas high school kids, and he came out first."

He learned to relax. He learned to see his goal—how to throw the discus—and, in a few months' time, he became a champion.

Why throw a discus? You might hurt somebody. Instead of discus, instead of running, why not take your self-respect? Make a project of it. Make it a beacon. Make it the shining light of what you can be. Not just any time. In crises, too.

Overcoming Crises

The main theme of this chapter is how to surmount the many crises in your life and go on to rich, rewarding experiences.

This is easier said than done.

Still, if you apply yourself properly, chances are you can do it.

We have, in the course of dealing with this subject, dwelt upon inner dignity and senseless violence, upon the overcoming of frustration, upon peace of mind and the winning out over fear, as well as upon the proper channeling of aggression. All are relevant to the manner in which we deal with crises, and to whether we survive crises and go on to growth experiences or whether we let the crisis conditions overwhelm us and plunge us into a failure cycle that might become a rigid, tortured life pattern.

During the time I was writing the material for this chapter, a great man, Senator Robert Kennedy, was killed in an act of senseless, destructive violence. This shocked us all. Coming as it did on the heels of the equally tragic slaying of the great civil rights leader, Dr. Martin Luther King, Jr., the shock was overwhelming. Both men were sincerely constructive in the ways they lived. They died at heartbreakingly young ages; yet, while they lived, they lived richly.

They left messages for us who survived them: that we human beings must live and strive to fulfill ourselves. That we must meet crises head-on, refusing to buckle under to the forces of crisis, but overcoming crisis with the power of our determination, the sincerity of our intentions, and our reliance on an inner dignity and self-respect that will not fade away with the changing winds.

You can not avoid crisis—except by hiding under your bed all your life and refusing to come out and meet the world. And this is no answer.

Therefore, you must resolve to win out over the many, inevitable crises in your life. I hope that my suggestions in this chapter will help you. I believe they will.

And your winning out over crises is a major step in your major battle—the confrontation and final victory over the forces of frustration.

Raymond Charles Barker

Dr. Maltz and I have placed great emphasis on self-respect, self-confidence, self-control, and the need for being a self-fulfilled success person. We have stressed the importance of your self-image—what you see when you look in the mirror. Notice how the word *self* appears in each of these attributes. That is because *your self* is the only significant entity in your world.

We have also been compassionate, we hope, as we have tried to explain that perfection—or even near perfection—is something that few of us attain, and we certainly don't do it over night. You will always be an evolving, unfolding individual because that's what you were created to be, and each time you aim for a new goal you will run into new obstacles. You will continue to be a mistake-maker and a mistake-breaker. As you move forward, remember that *your* self-expression is the self-expression of the Intelligence that created you. You need the challenge and the excitement of constant change in order to function as Divine Mind intended that you should.

While you have been reading this book, you have been learning to accept yourself for what you are, an intelligent being with various weaknesses and strengths, who is living in a today world and who is capable of setting sights on a creative tomorrow. You also have been developing a *mental balance* that is your birthright. But since you are a self-willed person you may have sacrificed some of that balance along the pathways of experience and growth. You have learned that by controlling your thoughts and feelings in a way that enables you to

139

reach both minor and major goals, you can establish your own measure of mental health.

Mental health is the most priceless commodity that you can possess. You were born to have it because you were created to be a center of intelligence in the one Creative Mind. You also were born with free will and therefore your life has developed according to your own patterns of thinking and feeling. Your degree of mental health right now determines the ease with which you are able to face and solve problems.

Dr. Maltz has made it clear that the aim of the science of Psycho-Cybernetics is to help people attain mental health as they conquer their frustrations. Our teaching of the Science of Mind achieves the same thing; to help those interested in this science to recognize themselves as *mind in control of every situation*. This means having faith in oneself as a spiritual being who is an individualization of the one Infinite Mind.

Largely without any spiritual connotation, the importance of mind and its functions is being recognized in many fields of research today. You and I are fortunate to live at a time when much thought is being given to the operations of the mind and emotions and their influence on our bodies—on our failures, and on our successes. The broad subject of mental health is now one of national interest and concern. Psychologists, psychiatrists, and other specialists in the field are pressing forward in many areas of research and clinical investigation. They are gaining new understanding of the various phases of human behavior as they relate to the workings of the mind.

These are some of the down-to-earth questions being asked: Why do mentally disturbed people do what they do? Why do they say they feel as if they are "falling apart," or "going to pieces" or "losing their balance"? Why does mental illness affect people at all economic levels? Why do many patients whose minds aren't functioning properly recover in a short time, while others need prolonged understanding and care? Trained psychotherapists are asking what more we can do to help these disturbed people.

Early in this century a person who had a serious

"mental breakdown" was usually considered insane and put away in an asylum. His case was considered hopeless and with this grim prognosis he was left to deteriorate and eventually to die. In contrast, many of today's psychiatrists suggest that relatively few cases of mental illness, or mental dysfunction, should be labeled incurable. Today's goals include learning how to prevent as well as how to cure varying degrees of mental disturbance.

In the field of medicine, too, we find an ever-increasing awareness of the mind's influence on the body. The terms *psychosomatic illness* and *psychosomatic medicine* are well known to most intelligent laymen. It is fairly common knowledge that disturbance of the mind and emotions can cause peptic ulcer, high blood pressure, migraine headaches, arthritis, trouble with eyesight and hearing, and all sorts of other disagreeable ailments. But any idea that the subconscious mind, acting in a destructive way, could cause such a universal ailment as the common cold would have been considered revolutionary —practically unbelievable—less than a century ago. I read some shocking statistics about the common cold some years back. Let me quote them to you.

"Americans will spend Three Hundred and Fifty Million Dollars ($350,000,000) on the prevention and cure of the common cold during the year 1963." This statement, from market research authorities, was published in *Forbes Magazine,* March 1, 1963.

At about the same time another research report showed that 22,800,000 Americans went to medical doctors in a single year to be treated for the common cold—22 percent of these sufferers made at least a second visit to the doctor.

These figures startled me. I did some thinking about the number of days men and women lose from work annually because of the common cold, the financial losses to corporations for these lost man-hours, and the cost to insurance companies for temporary hospitalization.

All of this, to my mind, is a needless waste of time, energy, and money. I am well aware, after thirty years' experience in the field of spiritual mind healing, that the common cold and its fellow complaints—virus infection, sinus troubles, post nasal drip, and similar ailments—will yield to spiritual-mental treatment.

As a result of my thinking on this subject I have published a booklet entitled *The Cause and Cure of the Common Cold*. In it I explain that colds do not come from material or external causes. The weather does not cause colds. Overwork and fatigue do not cause them. Exposure to others with colds does not cause them.

There is only one cause of the common cold. It originates in the mental-emotional constitution of the individual. It is an outer expression of an inner hurt. When you know this and are able to admit to yourself that your mind and emotions alone have caused the cold, you can be cured by the spiritual ideas and spiritual treatments we have been discussing here.

If your mind and emotions make your body sick, you may be sure that the self-destructive forces in your subconscious, which both Dr. Maltz and I have already discussed to some extent, are at work. These forces seem to be present to a greater or lesser extent in each of us, but the destructive urge is rarely aimed at total destruction. An obvious exception, of course, is the person who commits suicide. Less obvious is the self-destructive subconscious aim of an individual who "worries himself to death," or the one who claims that he is "killing himself with overwork," or the person who allows himself to "pine away from loneliness." We have many common expressions of that sort that have a deeper significance than the one that is generally accepted on the surface.

Anyone who indulges in fears without trying to erase them from the subconscious is being self-destructive. Anyone who repeats a problem over and over again without trying to find a solution is being self-destructive. Anyone who nurses a grudge or allows himself to feel resentful is being self-destructive. He is not hurting the person he resents. He is harming himself.

Persons who have set their sights on the failure side of life are likely to experience the emotions I've just mentioned. They need to do something immediately to get over onto the success side. They can't do it through long worry sessions or by falling into states of deep depression. If you want to keep your mental health, stay on the optimistic side of life. This doesn't mean that you should adopt a "happy-go-lucky" attitude. It means that happiness and success come to you when you *know and believe* that they are yours, because you have made a decision to have them.

I have frequently had someone say to me: "I think I must have been born a pessimist." That's not true. Neither you nor anyone else is born a pessimist. The chronic condition may arise when you, as a child, are consistently discouraged by one or both of your parents; by other children; by your teachers; or by gloomy people with whom you come in contact. Their unhappy outlook is assimilated by your immature mind. From childhood on, after you've been under this negative influence, you never expect anything to turn out right. Since there is a universal and immutable law that operates to provide us with what we expect to get, nothing does turn out right for you.

As a responsible adult who wants to live a full and joyful life, you need to do something to correct your pessimistic attitude. Change your expectations. Expect what you want, not what you are afraid will happen. You can't change *quickly* from pessimism to optimism, but *you can do it*. Try being optimistic on just one subject at a time; make it one subject a day; one subject a week; or, if it is necessary to take more time, be optimistic in one situation once a month. Develop the habit of optimism.

Pessimism and depression are symptoms of an underlying subconscious danger. They indicate that something is wrong with your mental health. If you continue in these negative emotional states, you are automatically indulging in an act of self-destruction. Now is the time to catch yourself and control your thoughts and feelings. It is time for decision. You cannot conquer any negatives until you decide to do so.

Decision opens the door to new ideas. But the door doesn't open to the pessimist or the depressed person until he makes up his mind to have no more self-destructive nonsense in his life. This is because within you there is an Infinite Knower who can only *know* when your mind is operating affirmatively. Great ideas do not come to pessimists.

You may say: "Well, I knew a man who was an inventor, and he was a pessimist, but he got ideas all the time." This may be true. He got ideas in the area about which he was enthusiastic. This was at the point of his invention. He was affirmative in the area of his inventions, therefore he got ideas that helped him carry them out. He did not get creative ideas in any other area. When he wasn't inventing he was a pessimist declaring that the world was "going to pot."

I often have people try to tell me how terrible it is to live in New York City these days. I say to them: "Why don't you move? Try Albany, Schenectady, or Hartford, Connecticut." But they don't want to move. They're just complainers who want to harp about something that's wrong. I say to them: "Sit down and make a list of six things that are right with New York." This provides an affirmative mental action which invites new ideas.

The self-destructive instinct tends to remain inoperative and ineffective when you are in a good mental health state. It begins its action only when you move to the negative side of mind. We move to the negative side too often, because we haven't yet trained our minds sufficiently to catch our errors in thinking and make the necessary corrections in order to keep ourselves beamed toward our positive goals.

You are the only person who runs your mind, and your mind runs your life. Therefore you are the only person who runs your life. You may declare that that isn't true. You may claim that a family situation runs your life, or a job situation does it, or a personal relationship does it. This may seem to be the case, but it is *you*, your mind, that is allowing a situation or a condition to control your reactions. You are granting permission to the situation or the condition so that it seems to run your life. If you don't take control, your entire existence will be run by the basic patterns already in your subconscious mind. These, at best, will probably be average or mediocre and your life will be average and unfruitful. You will experience frustration and failure.

I have had people say to me, "Dr. Barker, I live just for my work." That's not mental health. I've heard mothers say: "I live just for my family." There is no need to do that. You have to be you. This doesn't mean that you won't do your work if you are a worker; it doesn't mean that you won't look after your family if you are a mother. It means that you are an individual. You are not to be absorbed into a situation. You are always to be the director of a situation. This means self-responsibility. You have to take complete responsibility for yourself in order to be what Divine Intelligence expects you to be.

Dr. Maltz has used the expression: "Police yourself." You do this not by watching your actions. You do it by watching your mind and keeping your thoughts on your destination. The purpose of a police force in any city is to maintain order. That is its primary function. Its secondary functions are the seeking and finding of people who break the laws of order. But the original concept of a police force is that of a body of individuals whose purpose is to keep order.

You "police" yourself when you keep your mind in order. Mental order is mental health. We have an old-fashioned expression that says: "Cleanliness is next to Godliness." But order is the first law of the universe. Behind every successful individual there is order. Behind every creative mind there is order. I do not believe that anyone can have a sense of well-being in life without order. That's what I call policing myself. I see to it that *my mind* is in order; that *my affairs* are in order; that *my home* and *my office* are in order; and that *life itself* is in order for me.

Some years ago, I knew a noted clergyman who, once or twice a year, would tell his congregation that everyone should have a will—a last will and testament. It is interesting to note that when he died he didn't have one; so, obviously, he didn't practive what he preached.

Failure to have a proper will indicates that the person who fails to do this dislikes his relatives. He wants deliberately to leave a mess for other people to clean up. Remember that, and "get thee to the lawyer on time." Don't worry about getting to the church on time, as the familiar song admonishes—just get to the lawyer on time.

My seeming digression here isn't really a digression at all. Making out a will is only one of the many steps in the entire process of setting your mind and your affairs in order. Keeping your home or apartment clean and uncluttered is a matter of personal orderliness. Keeping your clothes clean and pressed and your shoes shined is another, and so is keeping your bank account straight. Developing a habit of personal orderliness in every area of your life is vital to your success.

Keeping an orderly mind is even more important, althought I consider that orderly living and an orderly mind are just two sides of one coin. As you set your mind in order you may have to get rid of a lot of mental rubbish. Get rid of petty feelings of dislike; of condemnation; of being upset by trivialities; of being confused in your thinking; and of being unable to reach decisions. Learn to take a stand on what you believe, or do not believe, and follow through on what you decide.

A successful man does not worry in the field in which he is a success. He may worry about his wife's illness, or his son's failure to get through college, but he has self-confidence when it comes to matters related to his own career. He knows that the problems there arise to be solved, not to be contemplated. That is an important statement for everyone to remember. *The problem appears in order to be solved.* It does not appear to be lingered over, to be mulled over, or to be assimilated. It appears in order that a solution can be called out of the mind of the individual experiencing the problem.

Solutions are not plucked out of thin air. They do not come from your next-door neighbor or from the policeman on the beat. They come from the Infinite Knower within you. I do not believe that a problem ever arises in the life of any individual without the answer being available *before the problem arises.* We often speak of the law of supply and demand. Problem solving involves this law, and please note that the word supply precedes the word demand. I believe that the answer to any problem in my life is in my mind, as the problem appears, waiting for me to call upon it; to use it and thereby solve the problem.

I believe that the individual mind individualizes the Divine Intelligence. Therefore, I believe that the Knower in you knows what you need to know at the instant in time that you need to know it. By policing your mind, you solve problems that otherwise would bring various forms of frustration into your life. Frustration keeps the mind cluttered and disorganized and prevents the Knower in you from being able to reveal what you need to know. In other words, you can't reach a constructive conclusion about anything if your mind is completely occupied by useless and destructive thoughts.

Dr. Maltz stressed the necessity of what he called the *dignity of self-belief*, the dignity of having accepted yourself as a creative individual.

Once again, some person will say: "But I haven't done anything creative in my life. How can I accept myself as a creative person?" First of all, it is impossible to have lived to the age of twenty-one and not have done something creative. But we won't dwell on that. As counselors we help the person who consults us to get started on something creative in his life—something simple. Here we go back to the importance of seeking a goal. Let the person select what he wants to be or wants to do; then help him, through the use of spiritual knowing and positive thinking, to move ahead. It is vital for everyone to accept himself as a creative person, valuable to himself and to the world.

The pessimist, of course, will say: "The world would never miss me." In his present state, that's quite true. He wouldn't be missed unless folks started noticing how much happier they felt when he wasn't around. In a short time he probably would be forgotten.

But that isn't the point I want to make. You need this world as long as you are in it. You need to function effectively in this world as long as you are in it. You cannot function effectively without self-belief and it must be self-belief of the right kind. The most negative person alive has self-belief, but it's on the wrong side of the track. He unconsciously has accepted himself as being no good.

This is self-belief that must be uprooted and replaced by a conscious belief in your creative value in your present world. You run your world. I run my world. I am the only thinker in my mind. I am the only person who can discipline my emotions. I am the only person who can channel my emotions into success patterns. Others can advise me. But I have to do the work myself.

This pattern of creative self-belief is the Dignity of Being. I am putting a capital "D" on Dignity and a capital "B" on Being—the Dignity of Being in existence at this time. You and I were born to live this year fully, and all of the years to come. We were born to live them, not in part but in full. This means creativity in every level of your experience.

Many people are creative at work but noncreative at home. Many people are creative in the arts and noncreative in their personal relationships. When you have achieved creativeness in every area of your present-day life, you have made the conquest of boredom.

I am always astounded at the people who exist, in the midst of life today, who are bored—because we are living in exciting, interesting, changing, and provocative times.

I am glad I wasn't around for the Revolutionary War. I am glad that I am right here, right now. I am going to be in this world, and since I am going to be in it, I am going to police my thinking so that I will have a mental health that will enable me to enjoy living. I do not intend to sit around in my present world remembering past experiences and becoming frustrated. I am going to be spirit in action every waking moment of my life.

The world was not created for people who want to remain in a rut, even if it is a comfortable and profitable rut. Dr. Maltz could have remained an excellent, highly reputable, world-renowned plastic surgeon and nothing more. If he had followed that pattern, I suspect that the last years of his life would have been filled with boredom. But he didn't remain so. An *idea* hit him. He went to work on it and he worked intelligently. Today he is far from being bored. He lectures everywhere, goes everywhere, does everything, and rejoices in everything. I use him as an example merely because you have been reading what he has to say.

He has mentioned uncertainty, though not in the way I am going to discuss it. The law of life always has been and always will be uncertainty. There are no finalities; there never have been and there never will be. Everything is uncertain—that's why everything is interesting.

The saddest people in the world are those who have made certain every area of their lives. They live by routine, they think by routine, and eventually they probably will die in a routine way. These people believe in the walls they have built around themselves; they feel safe because they believe these walls protect them from uncertainty. Of course, all they have done is to put themselves into their own mental jail. They have refused to face up to the fact that everything is uncertain; everything is flexible; and everything is changing.

I can live in uncertainty. I can live with it. I can rejoice in it, because I know that uncertainty means there is always going to be a fresh experience for me.

The uncertainty of a world situation doesn't frighten me. This is because every problem that appears reveals its own answer. The negative reveals its own affirmative, according to the law of opposites. Where there is black there is white; where there is short there is tall; where there is thin there is fat; and so on. And when things seem static there is bound to be change.

It is absolutely normal to be uncertain. But you don't flounder in uncertainty; you direct it. You view uncertainty without fear. Everything in my life will be uncertain and changing for the rest of my days and I intend to direct my uncertainties all of the way.

I do not want the boredom of certainty. I want the excitement of uncertainty. I want all the discoveries that go with uncertainty. This is because I do have the dignity of self-belief, the creative, constructive aggression that Dr. Maltz has talked about. Aggression used rightly puts us farther along on the road to success; used incorrectly it gets us into all kinds of trouble. My aggressiveness is born of self-belief. That which I am, I express fully.

I impose nothing on other people and if you have true mental health you impose nothing on other people. If you run your own life, you have ceased to have any desire to run other people's lives. I, personally, have granted a declaration of independence to every loved one, friend and neighbor. They are free. If I don't like what they are doing, I say nothing; because they are free to do it. But I also am free to do what I want to do, as long as it does not interfere with the good of another soul.

Too often, however, we sit back and say: "Well, I don't want to hurt anyone." We continue to put up with nonsense. There is nothing in the *law of man* or the *law of the spirit* that demands that anyone should put up with nonsense from other people. Jesus certainly did not do it. He told off the Pharisees every time he got a chance. He let them know exactly where he stood, and they knew where he stood. They knew that here was one man they could not control. The reason they couldn't control him was that he was in control of himself. When you are in control of yourself, other people can't control you.

Here is a factor of great importance to you in your use of self-control. *Reduce your pressures.* Check to see how many false responsibilities you are carrying around. It is human ego to believe that the whole world depends upon you. If you find yourself saying: "I have so many responsibilities," reduce them. Pressures beyond a certain point will wreck your mental health.

When I ask some "overburdened" person why he feels overburdened, he frequently says: "I take on everybody's problem." My answer is: "I don't—*I don't.*" I am sympathetic, in the right sense of that word. I have compassion. But I can't take on anyone else's problems. I know of no one but myself whom I have ever worried about all night.

A critic will say, "That is selfishness." It is not. Every once in a while I look over my load of pressures and say, "Which one of these can I reduce to nothing?" You and I do so many things we really don't need to do. We do them because the world expects us to. Often I make a checklist. I ask myself: "Why am I doing this? Because I really want to?" Fine. "Because the world thinks I should?" No.

When you are enthusiastic about doing something, no pressure is involved. Any action of yours may become a pressure only when it comes under the heading of *duty* —one of the most unpleasant words in the English language! When a person says, "I've got to do my duty," I always know that he is going to do something he doesn't want to do. He is going to do it in a negative mental attitude. The act of duty won't help the receiver, and it will only turn the giver into a minor martyr.

One of the most insidious attitudes that can be inculcated in the human mind is that of *martyrdom.*

Looking back at the woman who said to me: "I've given my life for my family." I repeat my reply with stronger emphasis. I said to her: "You shouldn't have. You should have kept your individuality. You should have carried out your own private plans and raised the family at the same time." This is what any creative mother does. She does not submerge herself in her family. She runs the family but she retains her own fields of interest and keeps them alive. She doesn't desert the family; she handles the family and keeps her own creative interest alive.

Your situation is much the same. Your duty is only to your own mental health. Your duty is only to yourself —to be yourself, to love yourself, and to express yourself. Don't worry—when you are able to do this, you will make a contribution to the world. You will make a far greater one than you can make if you are in a morbid negative state. You will make a valuable contribution to your loved ones, your friends and your business associates. All of these people, basically, want you to be happy. The only way you can be happy is by accepting your right self-image. Love yourself and continue to be yourself. Then you can create.

The genius of Jesus was that he had accepted and announced his own self-image. There is no word anywhere in the Gospels that indicates that he, at any time, disliked himself. He knew who he was, accepted who he was and projected who he was. I believe we can say that he was a successful man.

When you do the same thing—and you have probably done it already—you are wonderful. You are wonderful not because of human ego. You are wonderful because that's the way life made you.

VI

On to Success!

Maxwell Maltz

In attacking our goal, the conquest of frustration, we have, of course, studied the question of frustration and illustrated the nature of frustration so we might better know our enemy.

But we have done more than this. We have also studied the importance of goal-setting. We have thought about the importance of your self-image. We have gone into mistake-making and mistake-breaking, into the acceptance of error in ourselves, into the tyranny of conscience and the healing ability of compassion. We have discussed the constructive and destructive outlets of aggression. We have analyzed happiness and unhappiness. We have made a number of pertinent observations about the human condition.

In short, we have tried to point the way to the good life—to the overcoming of frustration and failure.

Now, suppose that we take that final giant step—and discuss the whole concept of success as a way of life.

In a sense, this is automatic. When you conquer frustration, what can have you then? Success! Right? It is so obvious.

And yet, is it? Are you ready for success? Do you easily think in terms of success? Can you handle success? What threatens you more, success or failure?

This is truly a cloudy, complicated question. For the truth is that many, many people are not emotionally equipped to handle success.

Let me tell you a story a friend told me, for illustrative purposes.

It seems that, during World War II, he was an infantryman in Europe, a rifleman in a front-line American division fighting Nazi Germany's troops. It was late November, 1944, and in Alsace-Lorraine, around the French-German border, the Americans launched a big offensive. The fighting was fierce; the Germans retreated, but my friend's company, advancing, took heavy casualties—something in the neighborhood of 50 percent in the first few hours of the attack. They seized a key ridge and withstood artillery barrages. Soon the ridge was secured and they could rest.

But a few days later they moved through the countryside to a small village—their target. They attacked it frontally—and ran for cover as dozens of machine guns and rifles opened up on them.

Once again, on foot, after a short wait, they attacked. Jumping to their feet, they charged forward. Again, the German machine guns and rifles barked out; back they went, behind a slope which gave them protection.

Aidmen took the wounded back; the survivors, behind their slope, looked at each other, worried. What could they do? Attacking the village from their position was very difficult. Either they had to go up a steep slope, good targets for German sharpshooters, or try to pour through a narrow tunnel—even worse. And the enemy was most certainly ready for them.

Failure confronted them, certain failure. Even if they did capture this little village—which apparently consisted of one long street lined with houses—they would face destruction in the process. Few would live to tell the story of this one.

Perhaps a bazooka could knock out the nearest houses. The bazooka-man got to his feet to take aim, then leaped back. He was most fortunate, he was untouched—but there was a bullet hole in his helmet.

And so these American infantrymen looked at failure. They sent word back to headquarters. Then they waited.

Headquarters responded shortly. New orders. A new approach. And failure turned towards success. Destruction was avoided—with a new outlook.

A new approach. The infantrymen retreated back toward their own lines, then circled around toward the other end of the village. Here they moved in on the village from level terrain—the terrain was no longer such a handicap. The enemy did not expect them to come from this direction; they were not ready. And a tank called up from reserve completed the transformed picture.

In a matter of minutes, with this new approach, they captured the village and the surviving defenders were prisoners of war. Just like that.

One approach, failure. Another approach, success.

Now I don't tell this story to glorify war, certainly. I don't have to tell you that I loathe violence in all its forms.

But this story illustrates very effectively one of my key points—that your approach is of fundamental importance.

Just as these American soldiers had to decide on a success-type approach over a failure-type approach, so do you. So do you!

Not on the battleground that was Alsace-Lorraine, on the French-German border, but in the battleground of your mind.

For your mind is a battleground in which you win or lose, it is a battleground in which you decide on the nature of your approach to life, it is a battleground in which you lose the war against negative feelings or in which you win this essential battle and go on to face life with success-type approaches.

In each of our lives, we have to surmount unfavorable terrain every day—the problems and troubles and crises which are basic constituents of life. Sometimes we can meet the head-on; sometimes we must bypass them, reformulate our goals and move in from another direction. But we must gear ourselves to win with success-type approaches.

Now, let us analyze some of the obstacles which we set up to keep us from success.

The world is against you?

Well, sometimes it may seem to be, but chances are you will do all right with the world if you can first do all right with yourself.

You never get a break?

Again, some days you might not, but how about the others? In the final analysis, you make your breaks—

and the best break you can give yourself is to think realistically about how you can overcome the forces of frustration once and for all, as you take dead aim on success-type thinking.

You don't deserve success?

Now this is more like it—this is the type of thinking which bars the door of success to so many people—this is what we must discuss.

The Person Who Has No Rights

Are you a person who gives himself no rights? No rights in terms of success, fun, inner contentment? No rights in terms of anything?

There is such a person, you know. A person who feels such strong inferiority, such overwhelming guilt, such self-hatred, that he feels he has no rights, that he deserves no rights, that he didn't deserve to be born, and certainly that he doesn't deserve to live.

And, in truth, not just one person—many people. Many, many people who feel they have no basic human rights. So many suffering people who will not let themselves enjoy the only life they'll ever have. Perhaps they give themselves the right to own a car or a house or some other valuable material, tangible possessions, but they do not give themselves the right to feel successful, the right to feel worthwhile, the right to feel they are somebody.

Now let us suppose that you feel this way. You are always frustrated and this feeling follows like the night the day, for you always frustrate yourself. You worry about everything (worry will kill success as quickly as insect killer will kill insects). If you make a lot of money, you begin worrying about income taxes. If you're feeling healthy, you begin worrying about some disease a friend told you about. If you are humming and whistling as you pick up your morning newspaper, your face is creased with anxiety when you put it down.

Let us suppose you feel this way. You read about celebrities as if they were people from another planet. They're not, you know; they're people just like you and me. You find other people to admire and, in the process, you degrade yourself in any comparison. You find fault with your feelings; you find fault with your actions. You must be perfect; you must not make mistakes. You have no rights at all—you will not even allow yourself to be a human being.

What do you do about it?

You cannot allow yourself to continue to see yourself in such negative ways; if you do, you will always find yourself frustrated. You will make sure you fail—and you must see this—*you will make sure you fail because you are more comfortable with failure than you are with success.*

How do you change? How do you change from a failure-type approach to a success-type approach, as the infantrymen did?

I will now give you some suggestions to help you, but first you must realize the extent to which you refuse to give yourself rights, the extent to which you deny yourself rights that you would give most other people, the extent to which you are an enemy to yourself. Because unless you do this, and see that you are giving yourself a hard time, you will not want to change your approaches and attitudes. Why should you if you can't see that they are not working out for your welfare?

This may help:

Go back and re-read, in Chapter I, The Twelve Faces of Frustration.

Go over them carefully. Are they you?

Be honest with yourself. Are they?

If they are, chances are that you do not give yourself many rights.

If they are, chances are that you give yourself a pretty hard time. .

Now let's see what we can do to help you do right by yourself, rights-wise.

A New Success Approach

Let's see if we can't find a new approach to your thinking about yourself—a new approach to move you toward success.

The components of this new approach are not new.

We have discussed some of them, anyway. Still, this is a new approach for you, if it is not yet *yours*.

Make it yours, this old-new approach. Move to conquer frustration; move to approach success.

Our thinking is enlightened, and this is important. Bertrand Russell writes about how people in the Middle Ages, terrified during plague epidemics, clustered together in churches to pray to God, feeling that God, sensing their religiousness, would pity their plight and grant them relief from this dread disease. But their thinking was unenlightened. Objectively, they were harming themselves, for by crowding into the churches, at close quarters with poor ventilation, all they managed to do was spread the epidemic and bring on still more suffering.

But our thinking is enlightened, and we aim to rise above the epidemic of frustration on to a new success approach.

We talk the same language now, and it is a language aimed at moving us toward better living.

And here, in our language, are a few final thoughts so that you can cement the success approach we have paved for five chapters, so that you can rise above failure to success.

1. *Appreciate your individuality.* Too many people these days do not. Sometimes I feel a little cynical about modern "progress." *Max,* I say to myself, *when you were a kid, weren't people more themselves?* For, as a boy on the East Side of New York City, I knew a lot of "characters." And sometimes "characters" are just people who are not afraid to be themselves. They—the "characters" I knew when I was growing up—didn't have to take opinion polls before they felt, or thought or did something. They didn't care if everyone loved them —they were what they were.

Today too many people try to be someone else. To be successful, they feel they should look and act like some famous politician or movie star or entertainment personality. Then, they think, they will be successful.

But this won't work. You can not feel successful this way. The person who does this is a mass product, not a success. He is an assembly-line product, not a success.

You must learn to be yourself. You must learn to appreciate your own individuality. Don't sell yourself short! So what if you're not perfect! If you were absolutely perfect, no one could stand you. Other people would flee from you as if you carried a contagious disease. If you were perfection, you would make them feel inferior; you would remind them of their own fallibility.

God created you as an individual, not a robot. There is no one just like you—no matter what your faults or your assets, your wealth or your poverty, your opinons or your actions.

While you live, live—as an individual who appreciates himself as he is. You are genuine, the real thing —you are not an imitation. Appreciate your individuality! Accept your faults and your mistakes; emphasize your talents and your successes.

2. *Set goals every day.* It is the person who finds no purpose, no meaning in life who feels failure so intensely. You must make your own purpose . . . you must make your own meaning. No one else can do this for you.

Set goals every day. Every day.

So you know where you're going. Because you have to take your day and move it somewhere; you have to make your day live. Again, no one else can do this for you.

In goal-setting, the big mistake so many people make is to underestimate the importance of their goals.

"What can I do today?" a family man may say. "Make a little money, then come home and help the wife with the kids? What sort of goals are these?"

Excellent goals. Why underestimate them? So you're not a millionaire, so you won't be on television, so you won't save the universe single-handed, and you're not Superman or Batman, and you will not climb Mount Everest today. You're not a great hero—but you can be a good man, as a husband, as a father—plenty of worthwhile goals here.

"What can I do today?" a housewife may say. "I'll make breakfast, get the kids off to school, clean the house, make supper. Are these worthwhile goals?"

If they mean something to you, they are worthwhile.

If they mean something to you, you are a queen in your castle, you are a success beyond success.

Set your goals. Set them every day. Stop criticizing them because yours are not a millionaire's goals; think of the taxes he pays. Stop criticizing your goals because your life is not high adventure. An insurance company will issue a policy on your life perhaps, but not to the high adventurer. We must learn to live in reality, not fantasy. We must keep in touch with who we really are, not with the might-have-been.

3. *Keep after your goals.* In a sense, setting your goals is not enough. You have to keep after them. You must develop a persistence in realizing your goals—otherwise they lack meaning.

If you set a goal and fail one day, this is no failure at all. Life is not perfect for anyone; no one wakes up in the morning to a day in which every road leads straight to the realization of his goals. Life involves frustration, *but* it also involves the overcoming of frustration. Don't criticize yourself relentlessly if you set a goal one day and can not follow through to see its actualization. Keep after it. Set your goal for the following day, and the following day, and the day after that, until you have realized your goal.

You must not expect things to come to you. To achieve success, you must recognize that you must follow through. You must develop qualities such as patience, resourcefulness, and ingenuity, and keep your aggression efficiently channeled toward your goals. As in the story I told you, you may have to change tactics. The successful person, however, does not give up easily.

4. *Build your self-image.* And, finally, we come back to this. Because you can not be a success unless you are a success to yourself.

If you own your own house, you try to keep it in good shape. You mow the lawn, have the house painted, trim the shrubbery. You keep your driveway clear and do everything you can to enhance the value of your property.

Well and good. Enjoy your house, enjoy your car, enjoy all your material possessions.

But, above all, enjoy yourself—as you become a success to yourself. You can do this only as you build and build your good opinion of yourself, as you learn to see yourself at your best, as you see again and again your happy moments of the past, and work to make yourself the kind of person you always wanted to be.

You will not be a success if you mow your grass and trim your shrubbery, but neglect the building of your self-image, allowing weeds to grow.

You will not be a success if you make a million dollars but leave your self-image impoverished.

You will not be a success if you nourish and support a dozen children but leave your self-image starved.

In the final analysis, success *is* a growing self-image. More on this, now.

How to Build a Better Self-Image

1. s *Sense of direction.* If you have a goal, then you are going somewhere. This is the beginning of your great adventure in creative living. You try to improve your self-image, you take calculated risks to be better than what you think you are, you use frustration as a stimulus to rise above a problem, a mistake, a blunder, a heartache. Remember that negative feelings have value—to stir you on to overcome them . . . to reach goals within your capabilities, within your training. In other words, your goals must be realistic and within your limitations. And, when you have a sense of direction within your limitations, your opportunities for fulfillment become limitless.

2. u *Understanding.* To improve your self-image, you must understand that a mistake doesn't make you a failure. It is there to stir you on to rise above it. You must understand that you can not communicate with others until you learn to communicate with yourself. And then you have the responsibility to communicate with others, making every effort to understand them. This is the beginning of friendship—the growth of your self-image.

3. c *Courage.* You must have courage to take your chances in life. You must have the courage to start for another goal should you fail in one undertaking, remembering that success doesn't mean just being successful. More often it means the capacity to rise above a

blunder. You must have the courage to think creatively, then act creatively, refusing to be overcome by frustration because of momentary barriers or handicaps. You must have courage to jump the hurdle. And your courage reaches its greatest potential when you share it with someone less fortunate. Then your image is ten feet tall.

4. c *Compassion.* With compassion you're somebody; without it you are a failure. First, you must have compassion for yourself for you · are only human. And, equally important, you must have compassion for others, for it indicates your capacity to forgive. This means humility. This means maturity. This means a growing and glowing self-image.

5. e *Esteem.* You must appreciate your own worth as a human being. If you don't have self-respect, no one will give it to you. You can call a child on the telephone a thousand miles away and if he hears a whining voice, a voice of frustration, a voice without esteem, chances are that he will hang up on you. Unless you feel there is good in you, others won't find it. You must see yourself as a person whose destiny is to be happy. And when you fulfill yourself as a person with esteem—when you fulfill yourself with compassion for yourself and for others— you express the God-like quality within you. Your image is then in God's Image.

6. s *Self-acceptance.* Your image grows in stature when you accept yourself for what you are. Don't try to be someone else. If you try to imitate someone else, you are playing second fiddle to someone else's image. You are then behind the eight ball, a zombie living someone else's image; making your image shrink to the size of a microbe. Win, lose, or draw, you must be yourself at all times. You are neither superior nor inferior. You are *you,* a child of God, destined to overcome frustration only when you learn to improve yourself, improve your image, not someone else's.

7. s *Self-confidence.* Self-confidence comes from taking the calculated risks in living. You use the success instincts within you, you remember past successes, you use the confidence of past success in your present undertaking, refusing to let the negative feelings of yesterday sidetrack you from your goals. Confidence builds con-

fidence. Confidence can become a habit—like brushing your teeth. You can tap confidence then whenever you need to—instant confidence. You should be proud of your confidence; it is not conceit. The conceited person only pretends he is superior; he hides his feelings of inferiority. Confidence means humility, too—and compassion.

These seven ingredients spell SUCCESS.

The Twelve Faces of Success

Now let us look at The Twelve Faces of Success. Compare them with The Twelve Faces of Frustration in Chapter I.

1. *Truth.* Albert Camus, the famous French writer, said, "greatness consists in trying to be great." In the same way, happiness consists in trying to be happy, and success consists in trying to be successful.

Socrates said, "Know thyself."

Aurelius said, "Be thyself."

We say "forgive yourself." Try again. See the truth about yourself. It's not a bad truth. See your past successes; this, truthfully, is part of you.

2. *Imagination.* Imagination-plus means you have a goal within your capabilities and you use your mind to help you strive to reach this goal with constructive aggressiveness. All of us have imagination that we can make a habit of cultivating. Your imagination is destructive not constructive when you have no goals but move in circles, in merry-go-rounds of frustration.

3. *Relaxation.* You relax when you practice and live the four principles of relaxation:

a. Forgive others.
b. Forgive yourself.
c. See yourself at your best.
d. Keep up with yourself.

Relaxation implies that you set goals for your fulfillment. Relaxation means that you let your servo-mechanism, your success-mechanism, work for you under ideal conditions when you learn:

a. to do one thing at a time, with one thought at a time, one goal at a time.

    b. to live in the present, not in the past.

    c. to use your anxiety creatively to reach your goal.

    d. if a situation defies solution, to sleep *on* it, *not with* it.

    4. *The Aim of Happiness.* Happiness belongs to you, like your eyes, like your heart. See it refusing to let the tumor of doubt obstruct your vision. Feel the throb of your self-image anxious to win in life. Don't let it tick like a grandfather's clock in an empty room. Life is full of problems, but it's also full of excitement and joy. Reach for happiness without pushing people aside, and when you achieve happiness you have a moral responsibility to share it with others. And, remember, your first step toward happiness starts with a goal.

    5. *Good Habits.* You deliberately discard the bad habit of frustration for the good habit of confidence. All habits are forms of self-hypnosis—like brushing your teeth, eating your breakfast, or slipping into your shoes before you go out into the world. It is just as easy to have the good habit of compassion as the destructive habit of frustration. You make the decision; the responsibility is yours, no one else's. Stop seeking excuses for your errors. When you seek excuses, you avoid the achievement of goals, you sidetrack yourself from reality and creative living. A good habit here is to admit your errors and rise above them.

    6. *Accept Your Weaknesses.* In this way you have a floor under you when you come face to face with a problem, a crisis. You turn a crisis into an opportunity, not an opportunity into a crisis, when you accept your human frailty. Every day you are born again. Every day is a day of creative living. You dare not resign from life because you blunder. Don't give up the ship! You are a modern Columbus conquering the rough seas of frustration, accepting your limitations.

    7. *Compassion.* Compassion is the basis of successful creative living. You can not have a worthwhile goal without it. If you have it, through it the other aspects of the succes-mechanism will work for you. Through compassion you learn to overcome unproductive agitation, born of resentment—agitation that leads to elimination, where you walk away from life and turn your back on

your own identity, moving nowhere into the dark tunnel of your troubled mind. Remember the blackout in New York several years ago? Thirty million people were involved in a blackout beyond their control. But what about the many more millions of people the world over who create their own blackout through frustration, walking into the dark corridors of their own concentration camps that they build for themselves. Too often we see the dark world within our minds through a mistake. Ah, but through a little bit of compassion, a little bit of kindness for yourself, you give yourself another chance in life . . . and we all deserve another chance, another chance to walk back again into the dawn of a new creative day.

8. *Unmasking.* You stop wearing masks; you stop playing games with yourself and with others. How much energy is lost in this destructive process, a process of eating into yourself until there remains nothing of the great YOU that you can be. When you pretend you are someone else you withdraw from life, removing the vital fluids of your mind and spirit, leaving you empty as a human being.

You may wear sunglasses to protect your eyes from the sun. But how many of us wear sunglasses when we hit the pillow—I mean emotional sunglasses, to hide us from ourselves and from others while we try desperately to fall asleep. When you stop playing games with yourself and with others, you begin to play ball with your self-image. You stop hibernating and you live creatively, communicating with yourself and with the world—where you belong.

9. *Live Through Your Mistakes.* You cannot be a champion every day of your life. Like any athlete in sports who knows he can't win all the time, you must realize that you will not reach all your goals, and that if you reach most of them, you have become a champion in the art of living. You are not perfect and a mistake should not make you feel that you are inadequate; it should not fill you with frustration that forces you to retreat from life. Never tell yourself you are unlucky because you have failed in one undertaking, that people are inconsiderate and cruel. You are only cruel to your-

self then. A blunder should stimulate you to rise above it rather than to evade people; evade your commitment to be a full human being and you find yourself in a pit of despair and hatred.

10. *Never Retire.* You can never retire from life—whether you are three or thirty, six or sixty, nine or ninety. Every day you must live to the full, even if you are sixty-five and have to retire from your job. Those middle eight-hour periods before you go to bed—they are the precious hours of fulfillment, when you develop pursuits and hobbies that will make your senior years productive. You can not go into an artificial state of hibernation. It will only lead to despair. Have a goal every day, no matter how small.

I gave a seminar, a workshop in Psycho-Cybernetics in Monterey, California, and when it was over one man came up to thank me for teaching the course. He said: "Dr. Maltz, do you know why I took the course?" "Why?" I asked. And he answered: "I'm eighty-two and I'm practicing to be ninety."

11. *Consider Yourself a Winner.* Call upon your confidence of past successes; use this confidence. If you consider yourself a loser, you will be fearful and without enthusiasm. You will feel oppressed as if the air from your lungs had suddenly disappeared. This feeling of oppression prevents you from reaching your goals, blocking positive feelings and positive performance, leading to weariness, ennui, boredom. Do not let your strength flow out of you. Do not let your self-image shrink. Consider yourself a winner. Strengthen your self-image.

12. *Accept Yourself For What You Are.* You are neither superior nor inferior. You are a child of God, capable of blunder, capable of rising above it. Keep up with yourself, not with someone else. Nourish your self-image, not someone else's. When you look in the mirror, see the two sides of you—the person of frustration and the person of confidence. You can't stay on the fence of indecision. You must make up your mind who you want to be. Choose confidence. Reject frustration.

The Success Cycle

If you follow faithfully the suggestions given you in

this chapter and in other pages I've written, chances are you will sharply increase your ability to feel that you're a success.

Success usually leads to sucess—and on to more success. So that here you have another cycle. Not the destructive, heartbreaking cycle of failure, but a happy series of successes, a reactivation of your success-mechanism.

What a cycle for you! Truly a life cycle! Build it. Nurture it.

And more power to you!

All your life.

The Final Conquest of Frustration

So where have we gone on our little voyage of discovery?

To Europe?

No.

To the Caribbean?

No.

We have traveled to none of the portions of the globe; you will not find our destination on any map or atlas. No ships, no planes, no rolling seas, no cloud-filled skies!

We have looked inside ourselves to see if we couldn't find potent weapons for our conquest of frustration. For our final conquest of frustration.

And I certainly hope that many of you good people, reading and rereading my anecdotes and my advice, will find in these pages a refreshing tonic that will help you to rise above both the endlessly repeated cares of your everyday lives and above frustration itself as a way of wasting the life force that is so precious.

You, reading these pages—there are so many of you and of course you are all different in your ways. Your problems vary, your heartaches vary, your satisfactions vary, your life styles vary. For you are individuals, and, though you are the same, you are different.

Many of you, however, are similar, in that you have succumbed to a frustration that is perhaps a characteristic of our troubled times.

If my ideas will help you to rise above frustration—to happiness and success—then I will feel richly rewarded in my labors.

Then our voyage of discovery shall indeed have been fruitful.

The final conquest of frustration.

Raymond Charles Barker

You and I are goal-seekers, reaching our major goals through the step-by-step achievement of minor goals. We have set forth, in previous chapters of this book, the way in which we strive and attain our goals. You have already acquired an awareness of the need for self-examination, self-honesty, and self-acceptance. Now let's concentrate on one more need, another step we must take in order to maintain the mental and emotional balance that is our necessary equipment as we move forward toward personal success and personal happiness. This all-important step is presented here in the form of a question that requires your honest answer.

Have you the inner ability to face your fears?

We all have fears, you know. They may be little fears or big fears. Since we are, for the most part, subjective or subconscious beings, we may have fears that we don't even know about. Subconsciously, we tend to cover up and refuse to look at some of them, just as we often try to hide our mistakes instead of facing them and forgiving ourselves for them.

Many fears are unintelligent reactions. They are emotions out of control, operating without conscious reason. When we examine them more closely, however, we discover that some fears are two-sided. They are destructive if allowed to run rampant, but when properly directed they can often be used in a constructive way. We will go into this matter more deeply in a moment, but first let's consider a statement that Ernest Holmes, founder of Religious Science, made on the subject of fear:

171

Someone has said that the entire world is suffering from one big fear . . . the fear that God will not answer our prayers. Let us analyze the fears which possess us and see if this is true. The fear of lack is nothing more than the belief that God does not, and will not, supply us with whatever we need. The fear of death is the belief that the promises of eternal life may not be true. The fear of loss of health, loss of friends, loss of property— all arise from the belief that God is not all that we claim: Omniscience, Omnipotence, and Omnipresence.

"But what is fear? *Nothing more nor less than the negative use of faith* . . .*

Dr. Holmes, in the words just quoted, speaks of faith in God, the Infinite Mind; but in all of his teachings he also recognizes and proclaims the importance of faith in one's inner self. That is largely what I want to emphasize now.

If we have positive faith in ourselves, and in the Knower and Doer within, we can eventually harness most of our fears. If we place our faith in evil instead of good, however, we may remain fear-ridden all of our lives.

So let us ask ourselves in all sincerity: "Have I the ability to examine my emotions and recognize my fears for what they are? Am I willing to admit, without embarrassment or shame, that I have them and that I mean to do something about controlling or getting rid of them?"

Mentally and emotionally disturbed people who seek guidance from a professional psychologist or a psychiatrist are encouraged to uncover their fears and phobias and to learn how to cope with them. This, I believe, is one of the major accomplishments of the entire field of psychotherapy, the fact that the therapist's aim is to help the individual to know himself and to face himself.

It often takes time and patience to learn to know and understand why we are afraid in one area of conscious-

* *The Science of Mind,* Dodd, Mead & Company, New York, p. 156.

ness and completely undaunted in another. It frequently takes concentrated effort to remove *the mask* that Dr. Maltz refers to. Most of us try—at least now and then —to dodge the necessity of taking a square look at ourselves. That is not an intelligent way to run one's affairs.

I have known people who managed, however, to go right through life into their eighties and nineties without facing themselves. Some of them died with their masks on, so to speak. In so doing they failed to fulfill the purpose for which they were created and they missed the excitement of great and wonderful experiences.

The point I want to make is this: You live so much more comfortably with yourself when you know yourself, and you are able to live more creatively. You lessen your frustrations when you see what you are afraid of and try to do something about it. I repeat: Everyone is afraid of something now and then. Occasionally I find a person who says, "I'm not afraid of anything. I have no fears." That person either is a great liar or he needs to shake hands with himself and say, "How do you do! Let's really get acquainted."

You may believe that you know yourself thoroughly, but the process of getting acquainted applies to you, too. I believe you will find it extremely helpful if, within the next twenty-four hours, you will sit down and make a list of your fears, as you know them. It may not be a very long list, but I imagine it will contain some significant and some petty fears.

Most people have a fear about money, not having enough to live on. Fear of illness is not uncommon or unnatural. Some individuals are constantly afraid that there won't be enough time to get things done. Others dread nightfall because they are afraid they won't sleep, afraid they'll wake up in the middle of the night and lie awake for hours. Have you ever been afraid that you wouldn't live up to the expectations of someone you love or respect? Have you been afraid people would laugh at you? That they would snub you? Are you constantly afraid that an accident will happen to you or your loved ones? Are you afraid that you may be fired from your job? Do you spend needless hours *fearing the worst* about most of your life situations?

Be honest. None of these suggested fears may apply to you. If they don't, you will probably have some nerve-wracking substitutes.

As you look at your list, here is something to bear in mind, something I mentioned in an earlier paragraph. Not all fears are destructive. Some of them are constructive. They serve as goads to keep us going, to help us attain our goals. These constructive fears are actually basic drives that are necessary to the process of our development.

Let's take, for instance, the fact that many people save money simply because they are afraid they won't have it. The fear of not having enough money to live on is in itself a destructive fear. If you keep that fear uppermost in your mind all the time, you are setting up patterns of limitation in your subconscious and the result is that you will not have enough money. You are setting up a poverty pattern in your life through constant worry about lack. However, when you turn your fear of lack into a systematic program of saving, you are turning your destructive fear into a constuctive fear. You are responding to a sound basic drive instead of cowering in perpetual dread of a bleak tomorrow in which you expect to be very poor and very unhappy.

We mentioned the fear of illness. This may be an unreasoning fear. Aunt Julia may have developed crippling arthritis in her late forties; a friend or relative may have suffered a heart attack or died of a so-called incurable disease. If, after exposure to one of these experiences or something similar, you find yourself panicking at the slightest twinge of pain, and imagining that you are about to become disabled or die, you are giving way to a destructive fear. There probably is nothing wrong with you. Go to a doctor and have a checkup; find out.

When you know that you are essentially well, you can use your fear of illness in a constructive way. Instead of reacting to it with unreasonable emotion, let it help you develop some sensible habits. Let it be a drive that starts you sleeping the right number of hours, eating the right kind of food, and exercising as much as you should. It is possible that a person who is seriously frustrated in some other areas will stay well because he has been goaded into health by his fear of being sick.

The individual who is constantly under pressure for fear that he won't get some job done on time undoubtedly is a poor planner, or he plans to do too much in a limited time. Instead of being afraid that he won't be able to meet a deadline, he should let his fear point the way to better use of his time. Chances are that while he is trying to get one job done he is also worrying about the bills he hasn't paid, the promises he hasn't kept, and the things he believes he'll never be able to handle on schedule tomorrow and the next day. Remember we operate in a universe of law and order.

Fear of sleeplessness bothers a lot of people. Some try to handle their insomnia with sleeping pills. Others get up the moment they are wakeful and raid the refrigerator, perform some household task, or read a book. There probably are as many "remedies" for sleeplessness as there are sleepless people. Some of these remedies work; some don't. Did you ever stop to think that when you are awakened in the middle of the night it may be for a creative purpose. Perhaps there is a Divine urge within you that is presenting you with a great idea. Think about that a bit. Wonderful and inspirational ideas have come to alert minds in the middle of the night.

Those fears that stem from someone else's opinion of you, or reaction to you, are useless fears that should be replaced by self-acceptance and self-belief. I frequently offer this reminder: You are the only thinker in your world. You also are the only person who is living your life, and you are the only person who must be satisfied with what you think, what you feel, and what you experience. If you have a fear of accidents, you can turn it into a habit of reasonable caution. Fear of losing a job can be translated into an attitude of greater personal responsibility and dependability.

I feel reasonably certain that when you look at your fears, when you make your list and give it careful consideration, you will find at least some items that will offer you a basis for correcting your thoughts and feelings.

After you have made this self-examination, you will at least know where you are.

Compare this vital process of finding out where you are in your own livingness to the experience of finding your way on an unfamiliar road. You are lost. You look at the road map. You study it carefully and note the names of some towns, or the location of a river, pond or bridge. You drive along watching for some sign that you have seen on the map. Suddenly you come across such a sign and you know where you are. You are no longer lost, but you still must follow the road carefully in order to reach your destination.

On my way toward my goals, I examine the negatives in my consciousness. Then I take the necessary steps to change the negatives to positives. I look at every situation that seems to be negative, in order to see what I can do about it. I'm not concerned with what the nation can do; what the government can do; or what the city or state can do. I'm only concerned with what I can do. Once I see clearly what is wrong, I usually can see what I can do to make it right. If I refuse to see what is wrong, however, I can't do a thing to correct the troublesome situation or solve the problem.

We take the steps that lead to self-awareness in order to correct our aim and to set ourselves back on the right track when we seem to be missing the mark. We are fortunate in realizing that we can do this. People didn't always understand themselves so well.

As you no doubt are aware, most people are completely self-interested. They follow the trends and new discoveries in medicine. This gives them a knowledge of their physical selves. Tremendous strides in this field have been made since 1900. Tremendous strides also have been made in man's understanding of the mind and the emotions. It has even become fashionable for the layman to diagnose himself, using such clichés as the *inferiority complex,* the *anxiety neurosis,* the *split personality* and all the rest. His diagnosis is likely to be incorrect, but it indicates his interest in the subject of *himself*.

It is true that we know more about the physical body today than we have ever known in the history of life. We know more about how the mind and emotions work than we have ever known in the history of life. There also is something else of utmost importance that some of us know, but that not all people recognize.

This factor is the *spiritual side of life.* Dr. Maltz recognizes it; I recognize it; and many of you readers recognize it. We are the people who know, beyond any doubt, that there is a spiritual side to the mind and the emotions. There is a spiritual side to the physical body. We see a design; we see a plan. We see a something in us that will never lose hope. We see a something that will always spur us on and will always give us the "hunch," the idea. That something will always quietly say after any accomplishment: "Well done." *That is the way of the spirit in man.*

The spirit in man is that which makes you aware of evil in order to create good. It is that which stimulates you and says, "Keep on trying!" It is that which animates you as life. It is that which animates your consciousness as ideas, and that which animates your imagination so that you are always imaging yourself correctly.

The other day, without realizing what I was doing, I found myself worrying about an acquaintance of mine. Suddenly I stopped and said: "Wait a minute. I'm being unfair to that person." My worry wouldn't affect him, of course. But I was building the wrong image of that individual in my mind. Realizing this, I said to myself: "Let's get this straight. This man is competent; he has lived long enough to know what to do and he will do it. Anyway, it's none of my business."

Here was an instance where my vivid imagination was going in the wrong direction. We must not let such things happen. We need our imaginations, but we need them to further our own progress, not to fix wrong images of other people in our subconscious minds.

If you read the story of Joseph son of Jacob in the Old Testament, you will find that Joseph's father gave him a *coat of many colors.* This coat was a symbol of the imagination and imagination gives color to life. You are given the gift of imagination. One of its purposes is to help you envision yourself as you want to be. This is correct self-imaging. When you have seen yourself as you want to be, the next step is seeing yourself as already being that thing.

There is an ancient saying: "The ought to be is." In accordance with this statement, you first image yourself as you *ought to be*. Then you image yourself as *being*.

This is a success formula. I know of no books in the so-called self-help field, other than Dr. Maltz's and mine, which stress the importance of imagination as much as we do. I have proved the truth of "The ought to be is," many times in my own experience.

When we started plans for our new church building, which we now occupy with pride, we were faced with every possible difficulty. Difficulties with regard to finances and difficulties in connection with construction work.

I refused to be daunted. Each day I saw myself standing in the pulpit in the auditorium. This was in spite of the fact that at that time there was no floor. There was no ceiling. The designers had given me a picture of what the auditorium and pulpit would look like. They had shown me how the walls would look. They had shown me a sample of the rug and I knew that the chairs were being re-upholstered in the same color.

With these guidelines, I was able to stand before that pulpit—in my imagination—for about one minute a day. During that minute I visualized the complete picture as it is today. As soon as I had started this practice, which I should have started the moment we had the plans for the church, operations for its completion began to speed up.

I didn't find myself running around blaming labor for a strike dealing with delivery of steel. I did not accept as a problem the fact that certain beams couldn't be delivered. I just said: "Wait a minute. Practice what you preach, Barker." Then I would image myself in the pulpit and looking at the walls. I saw myself admiring the red carpet and looking at the seats upholstered to match. I saw the seats filled with people and imagined myself talking to them.

When I had practiced this imaging for a while, everything began to fall into line. When they told us we wouldn't be in the church by the first of March, I imaged some more. The contractors began moving the date back, and back and back. We moved into the church, which was fully equipped, on January first, not March first.

The situation I have just described illustrates the correct use of the mind. It takes courage to start such a procedure and to stick with it. But remember, anyone can wear the coat of many colors, his imagination. That is a part of man's natural heritage. I used my imagination to image the church that I wanted for myself and others. Then, using the maxim, "The ought to be is," I imaged the completed form, with myself and my audience in it.

This is an illustration of the unconscious success motivation. The church building was my success idea. We have success-motivation equipment and it responds when we have a goal and use the correct imagination. The mechanism moves into automatic action and creates out of our consciousness whatever we have taken as a goal. This is the mechanism which Dr. Maltz stresses in his book *Psycho-Cybernetics*. He explains that it can be used as a success-mechanism or as a failure-mechanism.

Again we see the similarity between some of the principles of Psycho-Cybernetics and those of the Science of Mind. There is one law of action, but we can use it in two ways. Similarly you can use your fears in two ways. When you clarify them and discover that most of them really are creative, you are ready to do your correct imaging.

At this point I am back to an old theme of mine, but I want to re-emphasize it. It is this: Investigate your potentials. You are greater than you think you are. You are far more intelligent than you think you are. You are far more handsome, if you are a man, than you think you are. You are far more beautiful, if you are a woman, than you think you are.

Your potentialities, regardless of your age, remain always the same. We are incomplete people seeking to complete ourselves. We are unfinished business and we always will be. We can't ever be finished because evolution won't let us be. Call it evolution, call it God, call it what you will—it won't let us.

Your potentialities are unique to you; mine are unique to me. But they are there and we should take a look at them quite often. Investigate the potentiality in you that will make you happy. I believe that everyone should be healthy, and happy, and prosperous. There is no virtue in illness and no virtue in sorrow or unhappiness. There is no virtue in lack. You were not created to bear a burden or to bear a cross. You were created to solve problems. Period. You were created to be happy in doing the problem-solving job.

Every problem you have actually is a blessing. It stimulates you to do new thinking, to investigate yourself a little more. Resolve that from here on, when a problem comes along, you are going to turn to the power within you and allow it to reveal the solution. It will do this through ideas. Your problem will be on its way to a solution as soon as you receive a new idea. Keep the channels of your mind open. As long as you are on the merry-go-round of worry and concern, repeatedly asking yourself *why, why, why,* nothing inspirational can get through. Ideas and solutions must have an open pathway into your consciousness.

Remember the importance of relaxation. When I'm looking for a new idea I sit very still. I relax and say: "Come on, mind, I need a new idea. You deliver it to me."

This probably is what the traditional church would call prayer. Just a few words spoken with sincerity and in complete faith. The Infinite is not impressed by long-winded petitions. Most clergymen pray too long. I do it quickly. I take only two minutes. I sit down, relax, and say: "Mind in me, you know what I need to know. Now give me my next idea so I can handle this problem." When I have finished that statement, I get up and go back to whatever I was doing. Soon the idea is revealed to me.

All of us have some unpleasant experiences that come into our lives. They often involve irksome problems.

They signal a time for action, action of a particular kind. Here is where we sit down and relax. Here is where we say: "Wait a minute. Life has never brought me a problem that I couldn't handle. It is not bringing me one now." That's what I call *faith*. I know that I can solve every problem because a spiritual idea is always revealed to me at the right time.

What do we mean by a *spiritual* idea? I have defined *spiritual* as intelligence in action. As I use the term it has nothing to do with piety. The universe is a spiritual system because it is intelligence an action. You are a spiritual being because you are intelligence in action.

Getting up in the morning and washing your body is just as spiritual as saying a prayer in a cathedral. It is intelligence in action. You have received this intelligence as a free gift from life. This intelligence is a universal intelligence, individualized in you, as you. Therefore, it has the right idea to solve your problem, to cure your frustrations, and to ensure your mental and emotional balance as you move toward creative goals. Your intelligence sparks your imagination.

You are well equipped, so use your equipment. People say to me, "Well, I have the wealth and the wisdom of past experience." I know that this is true, but it is not enough. You need the wealth of hope of the future. Anyone can relive past experience, but not everyone can create intelligent future experience. That is what you are going to do from now on.

If your future is dull, it is not Dr. Maltz's fault or mine. It is because you are too lazy to use the processes we teach. Remember, the solution to each of your problems is already in your mind, as potential. You don't find the solution by studying the problem. You find it by relaxing for a minute and letting the creative side of your mind go to work. When you *review* a problem you are using your creative process in a destructive way. But when you begin to think of the solution as being already in your mind, you move out of despair into hope. You cannot live without hope.

To me, hope is a creative expectation of a pleasant future. That is what all of us need. Do all of us have it?

Watch your friends. Watch their thinking; observe their manner of speaking. You will find that many of them do not have any real hope for the future.

Anyone can be a prophet of doom today. Anyone can look at world affairs, and the affairs of this nation, and say that civilization is headed for ruin. But I don't accept that verdict. I have creative anticipation. I believe that people in high places will take the constructive actions that are necessary to make this nation greater than it has ever been before.

Anyone can join the Mourners' Union. What we need is people who refuse to join. We need people with hope; people who know that there must be change, change that has its roots in you and in me. Most of the people who want the nation to change don't want to change themselves. They go on saying, "I'm all right." That's not true. No one is *all right*. We are partially right. We may be more right than wrong. But all of us constantly need some change. Otherwise we would be static people in a static world.

Investigate your potential for solving your problems, your potential for handling the everyday needs of living, your needs for happiness. God can do a lot more through a happy person than through a miserable one. Even if your life right now seems to be going along smoothly, remember your right to happiness. Expand your happiness. Be happier than you are. It's possible, you know.

There is another right I would like you to remember as well. That is your right to the correct kind of selfishness. I said the *correct kind* of selfishness.

I recall the case of a man who came to my office one day. He wanted me to give him a spiritual treatment for one million dollars. I asked him: "What will you do with a million dollars if you get it?" He replied: "I want to give it to my three children."

I suggested that instead of praying for one million dollars for this man we might pray for $350,000 for each of his children. He didn't go for that at all. His human ego would not have been inflated if we had succeeded in getting the lesser amounts for each of his children. He wanted that million dollars so he could *buy* his offspring later on. He wanted to be able to say, "Look what *I* gave you."

Gifts often carry *purchase power*. This man wanted purchase power. He wanted the million dollars only to exert power. This was selfishness used in a destructive way. I never saw that man again because he found out that I had no patience with this kind of nonsense.

There is another kind of selfishness that I recommend to you. It is a selfishness that you need if you want to maintain your own identity and to be the person you want to be. It requires that you adopt certain rules of self-preservation. *Don't let everyone walk all over you.* Have a certain point of self-privacy that cannot be invaded. You don't have to be an amateur do-gooder. There are enough professionals.

Don't let people rob you of your time. Time is a very precious element. In that connection, I am reminded of an eight-page letter I received in the office. It was handwritten, and I must say that the penmanship was very bad. I sent the letter back with a note informing the writer that if he would condense it to a single typewritten page I would read it and give him an answer. I am too busy to waste time on inconsiderate people, and so are you.

Here is a thought worth bearing in mind as you go through your day-by-day living. Whenever you can simplify your problem and state it clearly in one sentence, it is already half solved.

I started this chapter by saying that we are goal-seekers. Now I hope I have also made it clear that we are problem-solvers. We are problem-solvers when we let go; when we stop harrying the situation that bothers us and allow the Infinite Wisdom within us to come up with the right answer.

Here I would like to quote a pertinent paragraph from my book *The Power of Decision.**

"Your subconscious mind is a divine instrument. Its dexterity and precision will never be fully known. It is the greatest gift that you have. It is beyond price. It is

* *The Power of Decision,* Dodd, Mead & Company, New York, p. 180.

what you are as a creative individual. It accepts the impress of your thought and acts upon it. It knows neither good nor evil yet its processes can create both. Wise men have said that all creation is the result of the Law and the Word. The subconscious is the Law. What you place in it is the Word. This is the play of life upon itself."

Learn to *know* the precious equipment for living with which you are endowed. Learn to *recognize* the potency of your thoughts and feelings. Learn to *welcome* new ideas and have the courage to follow through with them. This is living. This is life. This is the purpose for which you were created. You were created to *be and become great.*